Cost-Benefit Analysis
of Quality Practices

IEEE

IEEE ⊕ computer society

⊕ CSPress

Press Operating Committee

Chair

James W. Cortada
IBM Institute for Business Value

Board Members

Mark J. Christensen, Independent Consultant
Richard E. (Dick) Fairley, Founder and Principal Associate, Software
    Engineering Management Associates (SEMA)
Cecilia Metra, Associate Professor of Electronics, University of Bologna
Linda Shafer, former Director, Software Quality Institute, The University
    of Texas at Austin
Evan Butterfield, Director of Products and Services
Kate Guillemette, Product Development Editor, CS Press

Cost-Benefit Analysis of Quality Practices

by Robert T. McCann

IEEE ReadyNotes Series

IEEE ⊕ computer society

⊕ CSPress

Page design by Monette Velasco.

ISBN-10: 0-7695-4659-5
ISBN-13: 978-0-7695-4659-9
IEEE Computer Society Order Number: P4569

Dedication

I would like to dedicate this work to my wife Carmen Lydia Lopez and my son Gregory Aidan McCann, for their consistent and continuing support in allowing me the time to think about the concepts and ideas necessary for this work to come together as an integrated whole. I would also like to acknowledge the foundational support I received from my father, George Ambrose McCann, and his father, Albert Edward McCann. They in particular provided me with early and consistent focus on processes, causal analysis, and continuous improvement per its initial publication by Frederick Winslow Taylor in *Principles of Scientific Management*. I also acknowledge my uncle John Edgar McCann, who demonstrated these values in various things he accomplished in his career, from founding a Little League organization that won a world championship to managing a bank. My cousin Thomas H. Witmer demonstrated these values as Chief Executive Officer of a corporation that ended up winning the Malcolm Baldrige award. My high school band director used these principles and the Army Field Manual to lead our high school band to several state championships and a world championship. Not least, I would like to acknowledge my thesis advisor Dr. Cecil Martin, Col. USAF, Ret., who taught me how to apply these values to software and systems development using the Software Engineering Institute Software Capability Maturity Model (now extended to the Capability Maturity Model Integrated) and who demonstrated the effectiveness of these models as contract Program Executive Officer by leading development of a very high quality development of a very large project that developed infrastructure and system function points equivalent to about 60 Million Lines of Code with very low cost and schedule variance and zero operational defects in several decades of operation.

The basic idea is that these principles have been around for over a century, are well demonstrated to work well, and work across many variant processes in multiple sectors of the economy. This author has had the privilege to know many people who have applied them successfully and has seen them work.

The author wishes to express deep and sincere appreciation and thanks to the IEEE Computer Society Press Operating Committee and editorial staff for their significant efforts in making this a more readable and useful document—especially Linda Shafer and Kate Guillemette. The examples in the first chapter would have been much weaker and less relevant without their deep interest and help in building that chapter.

About the Author

R obert McCann is a staff software engineer at Lockheed Martin Aeronautics in Fort Worth, Texas. He is currently an Institute of Electrical and Electronics Engineers Certified Software Development Professional as well as an INCOSE Certified Systems Engineering Professional and has nearly 20 years of experience in computational physics and high-performance computing, including nine years at Princeton Plasma Physics Laboratory working in the US Department of Energy-controlled fusion program, as well as about 10 years' experience in design and development of relational databases of various kinds.

Currently a member of the Lockheed Martin Aeronautics Metrics Working Group, Mr. McCann was previously a member of the Lockheed Martin IS&S Metrics Process Steering Committee. He currently works on logistics data flow process and logistics data design as well as improving organizational and project processes, methods, and metrics.

Mr. McCann has a Bachelor of Arts in physics with a concentration in mathematics from Shippensburg University, a Master of Science in physics from University of Maryland, 1973 (all but dissertation 1976), a Master of Science in computer science from Southwest Texas State University, 1996, as well as a Master of Science in Computer Systems Management/Software Development Management at the University of Maryland University College, 2004.

Contact information:
Lockheed Martin Aeronautics
1 Lockheed Blvd.
Fort Worth, TX 76108
Phone: (817) 935-4037
E-mail: bob.mccann@lmco.com

Contents

Chapter 1:
Introduction

This ReadyNote addresses the economics of rework in a process-oriented organization. Rework is the process of finding and repairing defects and is more costly the closer a project approaches the deployment of a product and likely to be even more costly after fielding the product. Recognizing that rework is an avoidable and expensive part of systems development and verification, one would expect organizations to strive to reduce it where possible.[1] The most expensive rework follows discovery of

---

1   On Cost-Plus contracts (see Setting Expectations at the end of this work), some managers view rework as equivalent to future sales and thus work to drive up costs by refusing to invest in quality. This approach is very near-sighted, of questionable ethics within the bounds of the Software Engineering Code of Ethics and Professional Practice (http://www.computer.org/portal/web/certification/csdp/ethics) and in the context of US DoD contracting under the Federal Acquisitions Regulation (Title 48 of the Code of Federal Regulations: https://www.acquisition.gov/Far/ as of 9/13/2011) for ACAT I and I-a

defects by the customer. Indeed, defects in some products can injure or seriously affect end users, resulting in costly law suits. Quality reviews such as inspections are known to reduce defects, but they have measurable cost to perform. Depending on the type of product and the quality level required, quality practices may be amended to reflect the appropriate amount of effort devoted to causal analysis, prevention, inspection, testing, and rework.

This business model describes a general approach to monitoring and analyzing rework costs. Once understood, this model provides explicit formulae to support an understanding of the cost-benefit analysis results.

Caution: *do not use a formula until after its derivation and meaning are fully understood!*

There are several necessary conditions for this model to be useful:

- First, there must be in place one or more quality review processes that gather necessary data.
- Second, from analysis of quality review data, there must be a realization that rework costs are a significant percent of overall project costs.
- Third, there must be a clear and present desire to study the economic advantages of reducing rework costs, and a willingness to pursue cost modeling.

Organizations that rank Maturity Level 3, 4, and 5 on the SEI CMMI organizational maturity level index are prime candidates for this disciplined approach to quality. That level of discipline is a significant enabler for this approach; however, less mature organizations may still learn from the approach and put in place quality review processes and data gathering activities in order to be poised to conduct the same modeling exercises once the adherence to those processes has yielded sufficient data to support the model and provide confidence in its calculated Return on Investment (ROI).

---

contracts, and possibly illegal on some contracts subject to the US Truth in Negotiations Act (10 USC § 2306a, 41 USC § 254b). At the very least this approach weighs against potential repeat business. Deferring some low priority or less important features from development to a post-deployment contract should be honestly negotiated with the customer with clarity; there are benefits to the Operations & Maintenance contract for doing so, for instance: skills retention, training, and stable staffing for the Operations & Maintenance contract. Dr. Watts Humphrey mentioned this issue shortly before his death: see his penultimate article in CrossTalk, page 11, at the top of the center column: http://www.crosstalkonline.org/storage/issue-archives/2010/201007/201007-Humphrey.pdf (as of 9/13/2011). His final article discusses other related management issues: http://www.crosstalkonline.org/storage/issue-archives/2010/201007/201007-Humphrey-2.pdf.

Why would any organization care about using this model?

First, appropriate use of this model can help an organization to be more competitive in the market by growing more effective teams. Second, this model can help an organization place its products into the market quicker and cheaper while delivering products that work well and do not just occupy shelf space in stores. Third, appropriate use of this model makes it easier to achieve high ratings on ISO-9000 and SEI/CMMI process assessments while lowering assessment costs.

Analyzing and mathematically modeling the cost of defect prevention and repair helps solve the problem of projects suffering high rework costs. It does so by modeling the effect of adding, dropping, or permuting quality practices and by modeling the payback of improvements to the verification processes employed.

Inspections of intellectual work products (e.g., requirements, architecture, design, code, plans, test scenarios, and test cases) in particular deliver an attractive return on investment and benefits in cost, schedule, quality, and customer satisfaction. Organizations that adopt inspection practices seek to prevent defect leakage that leads to costly rework. Many organizations now recognize the need for inspections, as empirical data on the success rate has been analyzed since 1976, when first published by Michael Fagan in the context of systems development.[2,3] More recently Michael Fagan's team lead, Ron Radice, published a book covering best practices that have evolved between the 1980s and the late 1990s.[4]

Data gathered from other organizations is no substitute for each individ-

---

2   M.E. Fagan, "Design and Code Inspections to Reduce Errors in Program Development," *IBM Systems Journal*, vol. 15, no. 3, 1976. Note that the inspection practice, although applied to software development, was actually developed for the full systems development context.

3   M.E. Fagan, "Advances in Software Inspections," *IEEE Transactions on Software Engineering*, vol. 12, no. 7, July 1986.

4   Ron Radice, "High Quality, Low Cost Software Inspections," Paradoxicon Publishing, 2001.

ual organization gathering local data by which to measure business performance. However, the adoption of work product inspections alone may not be enough for organizations that are mature or striving to become mature. Further culture change may be needed for the value of work product inspections and other quality practices fully to be realized.

Then, after inspections are institutionalized and data are gathered and analyzed, other questions arise, such as "how much inspection is enough?" At this point, mature (or soon-to-be mature) organizations may begin to create models by which to conduct "what if?" analyses leading to the refinement of quality practices.

This ReadyNote presents a generic model that determines the relative cost of interchanging, adding, or deleting quality practices and provides a statistically mature approach to estimating residual or latent defects. With respect to finding and fixing defects, quality practices typically follow a series: requirements inspection, design inspection, personal desk check, one-on-one peer review, implement and check, formal inspection, unit testing, identification of defects, repair/rework, re-verification, regression testing, causal analysis, planning and implementing process improvements, and more. Each step is time-consuming and therefore expensive. Project managers must decide whether they must conduct each step, as is often the case in critical systems (those requiring high integrity), or if they can drop one or more steps and still produce an acceptable product. Rather than experimenting on real projects (e.g., a random "try it and see" approach), a simple quantitative cost analysis model is a faster, less costly, and less risky approach to studying the necessary trade-offs.

To assuage any doubt of the seriousness of defect prevention and rework, the case has been made by several industry experts over the years, as is evident in the following paragraphs.

According to Dr. Barry Boehm and Dr. Vic Basili, the top 10 issues related to defect reduction are these:[5]

1. Developers take 100 times less effort to find and fix a problem than one reported by a customer.

---

5   R.W. Selby, ed., *Software Engineering: Barry W. Boehm's Lifetime Contributions to Software Development, Management, and Research*, Wiley-IEEE Computer Society Press, 2007. Note: the quoted "statistics" are low-precision heuristics. Actual performance will vary and will need to be measured.

2. Half of software project work is wasted on unnecessary rework. Current software projects spend about 40 to 50 percent of their effort on avoidable rework. Such rework consists of effort spent fixing software difficulties that could have been discovered earlier and fixed less expensively or avoided altogether. By implication, then, some effort must consist of "unavoidable rework."
3. Twenty percent of defects account for 80% of the rework.
4. Twenty percent of modules account for 80% of the defects and half the modules have no defects.
5. Ninety percent of downtime comes from 10% of the defects.
6. Peer reviews catch 60% of the defects.
7. Directed reviews are 35% more effective than non directed ones.
8. Discipline can reduce defects by 75%.
9. High-dependability modules cost twice as much to produce as low-dependability ones.
10. Half of all user programs contain nontrivial defects.

From *Critical Logic's Quality and Testing eLetter*:

> 50% or more of most software project costs go to repair and rework, not to original development work[.] Rework represents a huge avoidable cost. Unfortunately, [without a rigorous and comprehensive inspection program,] most of the need for rework does not become apparent until testing the actual software, well after specs are frozen and code written. This is the most expensive rework cycle.[6]

Quality Assurance, inspection, and testing processes to a large extent drive rework. Strong Quality Assurance and inspection procedures will find problems quickly, before the cost to repair skyrockets. When project quality assurance does not measure up, then too many problems go undiscovered until late in the testing effort—or worse, post-deployment. At this point, fixing the problem becomes expensive and time consuming. (However, there is a major management disincentive on Cost-Plus contracts, see footnote 1.)

---

6 "REWORK: Stopping Software Development Overruns," *Quality and Testing eLetter*, Critical Logic, Feb. 2007; http://www.critical-logic.com/newsletters/february07.html.

As William Ward wrote in the **Hewlett-Packard Journal***:*

> Rework cost is determined by the amount of effort and expense required to find and fix software defects during the integration through release phases of a software project. ... Software defect cost [includes] product profit loss [due to] missed market-window opportunities and the resultant loss of product sales. In other words, if a product release date slips because the software defect find and fix cycle is unnecessarily long, then potential product sales are irretrievably lost and overall lifetime profit dollars will be less.[7]

And a few years ago, GCN's Patience Wait reported:

> Every year the Government Accountability Office issues a report that gives a brief summary of the status of major weapons acquisition programs. And every year the reports say that many, if not most, of those acquisition programs are experiencing cost overruns and schedule delays in their software development segments.
>
> The problem is huge. In fiscal 2006, the Defense Department will spend as much as $12 billion on reworking software—30 percent of its estimated budget of $40 billion for research, development, testing and evaluation.[8]

Building an effective process performance model of quality practices can help project stakeholders determine how much effort should be spent on verification of defect-free products. An inappropriate amount will result in wasting precious resources, causing schedule delays and cost overruns or sacrificing the quality required for high-integrity systems. Under some cir-

---

7   W.T. Ward, "Calculating the Real Cost of Software Defects," *Hewlett-Packard Journal*, vol. 42, no. 4, Oct. 1991, pp. 55–58.

8   P. Wait, "Weapons projects misfire on software: Cost overruns constrict already tight budgets, GAO says," *Government Computer News*; http://www.gcn.com/print/25_18/41177-1.html (as of 9/13/2011). Note that the majority of these programs are Cost-Plus contracts.

cumstances, dropping a quality practice (e.g., no longer spending time on minor defects) is the right answer. Other circumstances, such as building critical systems, may call for adding a quality practice (e.g., implementing formal and semi-formal methods, inspecting all project artifacts; re-inspecting all rework).

Ideally, if product quality and process performance are program priorities, software development processes should be so advanced that no errors will enter a software system during development.[9] Typical practices only help to reduce the number of errors, not prevent all errors. However, even if the best practices were available, it would be risky to assume that no errors enter a system, especially if it is a system requiring high integrity. Nevertheless, according to Ron Radice, it is noted that some companies are routinely achieving 100% defect discovery with formal inspections in the context of mature continuous improvement.[10]

It may be difficult to catch all errors during testing, since exhaustive testing, which is testing of the software under all circumstances with all possible input sets, is not practical. **However, please note that, with use of the structure theorem for the part of the system implemented in prime modules, it is possible to do exactly that with formal methods and semi-formal methods such as inspections in time proportional to the total function points allocated to those prime modules.**[11] Without methods such as inspections, however, errors are much more likely to slip through. From the US Department of Commerce:

---

9   This author has previously worked for a company that prided itself on achieving a 70% success rate in delivering products that had zero major defects in the first two years of operations. Indeed, one such contract delivered a multi-million line software system within a half percent of the initial cost estimate and seven weeks ahead of schedule on a two-year contract, but another contract in the corporation had to return 18 months of acceptance testing budget because there was nothing to do! Due to corporate surgery, the executive who ended up holding both contracts in his portfolio did not reward this high performance. Instead, our Project Manager's career was effectively ended; he left the company shortly afterwards.

10   R. Radice, "Chapter 14," in *High Quality, Low Cost Software Inspections*, Paradoxicon Publishing, 2001.

11   C. Böhm and G. Jacopini, "Flow diagrams, Turing machines and languages with only two formation rules," *CACM*, vol. 9, no. 5, 1966. See also H.D. Mills, *Software Productivity*, Dorsett House Publishing, 1988, pp. 132, 119–120, 146–147, 158, and 16. See also R. Linger, *Structured Programming Theory and Practice*, Addison-Wesley, 1979, pp. 94–118 ('proper programs' is defined on p. 94, and the structure theorem is stated on p. 118).

If testing is the primary defect detection method, even a critical error may remain undetected and could be delivered along with the final product. This undetected error may subsequently cause a system failure, which results in costs not only to fix the error, but also for the system failure itself (e.g., plant shutdown, loss of life).[12]

In realistic systems development, it is reasonable to conclude that a combination of quality practices will be more cost-effective than use of a single method such as testing.

Who Should Care, and Why?

In addition to members of project development and test teams, this ReadyNote would be useful to members of organizations supporting project development and testing, such as

- project management,
- risk management,
- those participating in the systems and software lifecycle processes:
    - requirements development,
    - architecture,
    - design,
    - implementation,
    - and manufacture,
- those involved in verification and validation,
- quality assurance personnel
- system and software engineering process groups,
- and all IT/systems stakeholders, including clients and sponsors.

According to the US Department of Labor Statistics, the software field is large and growing. All of those involved would benefit from an understanding of this work:

---

12   W.W. Peng and D.R. Wallace, "Software Error Analysis," *NIST Special Publication 500-209*, US Department of Commerce, March 1993, http://hissa.nist.gov/HHRFdata/Artifacts/ITLdoc/209/error.htm.

- Computer software engineers held about 800,000 jobs in 2004. Approximately 460,000 were computer applications software engineers, and around 340,000 were computer systems software engineers. In 2004 this field was expected to grow much faster than average, increasing 27 percent or more.
- Computer systems analysts held about 487,000 jobs in 2004. In 2004 this field was expected to grow much faster than average, increasing 27 percent or more.
- Computer and information systems managers held about 280,000 jobs in 2004. This field is expected to grow faster than average, increasing 18 to 26 percent.

In truth, the largest stakeholders in the future growth in software and systems engineering will be India and China for all the right reasons. Both have large populations and are investing heavily in education and training of their future engineers.[13] Further, the cost of production in both countries is very low. That combination, together with a focus on quality, will create strong competition for software and systems development dollars in the world economy.

Cost Analysis of Quality Practices

A technically skilled workforce is not sufficient for competitive success. That workforce must be applied in an effective system of production. It is critical to understand the cost of production and the impact and effectiveness of the quality practices used in the business processes used to produce the systems and software that are to be sold. Indeed, the Capability Maturity Model Integrated (CMMI)'s High Maturity Practices are all about effective use of systems modeling skills to improve how we manage our work.[14] In the high maturity practices self-managed teams build process models of the characteristics that are important to success, and the team measures the process perfor-

---

13   India and China train roughly 500,000 engineers each year compared with 60,000 annually in the US. See "A New World Economy," http://www.businessweek.com/magazine/content/05_34/b3948401.htm (as of 9/13/2011): "As Cisco's Scheinman puts it: 'We came to India for the costs, we stayed for the quality, and we're now investing for the innovation.'"
14   See "Capability Maturity Model Integration," Wikipedia, http://en.wikipedia.org/wiki/Capability_Maturity_Model_Integration (as of 9/13/2011).

mance and uses the analysis results to stabilize and improve the performance of the team's processes. This approach is a natural evolution of the principles first discussed by Frederick Winslow Taylor in *Principles of Scientific Management, 1911,*[15] given the shift in the educational achievement of the workforce a century later from mostly illiterate (less than 6 years of schooling) to college graduates and beyond in the engineering and technology fields.

To model business performance accurately, it is necessary to train the employees to work according to documented repeatable practices, to encourage them to use such practices, and to check them for process compliance.[16] For the business models to be accurate predictors of costs, the processes must account for the majority of the activities performed by the assigned staff. Process exceptions and associated costs must be accurately recorded and causally analyzed. Then the results must be fed back into the planning process further to improve business performance. If the normal business practice is predominately ad hoc, the results will have significantly larger cost and schedule variances from initial estimates. For such a business to be successful and to remain successful in a competitive business sector, the processes must be capable of meeting business performance needs, and they must be continuously improved to stay ahead of the competition.

In what follows, this monograph will contain four primary chapters:

- an overall "cost of poor quality"[17] model sufficient to evaluate the cost-effectiveness of inserting quality verification and repair steps into an overall process flow
- a causal model of a generic quality verification and repair process
- an analysis of the cost-effectiveness boundary of the generic verification and repair process

15   F.W. Taylor, *Principles of Scientific Management,* Harper & Brothers, 1911.

16   The required paradigm shift can be a major cultural challenge for some employees who come from cultures where nearly everything is taken as directly personal and abstractions such as role playing are discouraged or punished. Phrases such as "I am what I do" are indicators of cultural challenges to process participation, and cultures that view acting, performing arts, and team sports as sinful also present cultural challenges to process participation. On the other extreme, Shakespeare's summary in *As You Like It,* Act 2, scene 7, 139–143, "all the world's a stage," neatly summarizes where effective process focus leads.

17   See H.J. Harrington, *Poor-Quality Cost,* CPC Press, 1987. See also "American Society for Quality," and "Cost of Poor Quality," both from Wikipedia (as of 9/13/2011).

- a model for estimating residual defects in products that have been subject to two or more independent verification and repair steps.

It is worthwhile to note that the model that follows can be applied to a wide variety of task networks via use of the task network equivalent of Thévenin's Theorem;[18] complex task networks can be idealized by equivalent simple nodes with the same inputs and outputs as the complex network.[19] The utility of this abstraction will become evident in the next chapter, in which a series of complex process steps is replaced by a simple graph network that models the flow of defects and the associated rework.

---

18   See "Thévenin's theorem," Wikipedia, http://en.wikipedia.org/wiki/ Th%C3%A9venin's_theorem (as of 5/11/2011).

19   J.C. Martin, "Chapter 7: Minimal Finite Automata," in *Introduction to Languages and the Theory of Computation*, McGraw-Hill, Inc., 1991, pp. 121-137. Of particular note is Theorem 7.3 on page 137: "If M1 and M2 are both minimum-state Finite Automata recognizing a language L Σ^*, M1 is isomorphic to M2."

Chapter 2:
The Relative Cost of Interchanging, Adding, or Dropping Quality Practices[1]

I n developing systems and software, there are multiple opportunities to perform quality practices to find and fix defects prior to putting the system or software into operation. This chapter demonstrates the following conclusions:

- In general, the quality practices should be ordered by increasing average cost to find and fix defects. Fixed costs do not affect this conclusion, but

1   Adapted from "The Relative Cost of Interchanging, Adding, or Dropping Quality Practices," *CrossTalk*, June 2010, pp. 25–28, http://www.crosstalkonline.org/storage/issue-archives/2007/200706/200706-McCann.pdf (as of 9/13/2011).

significant differences either in defect detection effectiveness or in the effectiveness of verifying rework-induced defects can modify the conclusion.
- One should retain/add a second quality practice, provided it is cost-effective to do so.

In the beginning of a new project, project management gets to decide a very important issue, namely what work products are subject to a verification process, e.g., peer reviews, formal inspection, testing, etc. Some work products may even be deemed sufficiently critical that they are subjected to multiple verification processes during the development lifecycle, e.g., requirements inspection, design inspection, code inspection, code desk check, compile and fix, informal peer reviews of various kinds, and various flavors of testing.

In these cases, there is nearly always a discussion of whether to use an informal peer review instead of a formal inspection, whether to skip the pre-compile desk check, and whether to perform the code inspection before or after the first successful compile or even after the completion of unit testing. What is always present is the persistent nagging feeling that too much or too little was spent on verification. This chapter, together with two previous articles on cost-effectiveness of inspections,[2] addresses that issue with a simple quantitative cost analysis model. It should be noted that this model is easily extended as causes of variation in any of the factors become known.

In what follows, statistical reasoning is used. *Where that is not appropriate, the results may differ.*[3] For instance it is highly unlikely that a compilation test will discover a design defect (such as poor choice of algorithm) that results in

---

2   "How Much Code Inspection is Enough?" *CrossTalk*, July 2001, and "When is it Cost Effective to use Formal Software Inspections?" *CrossTalk*, March 2004.

3   Organizations having well measured, repeatable practices will likely be capable of generating enough data for statistically valid analyses. CMMI level 1 organizations, not having repeatable practices and not having systematic process measurement, will likely find themselves less able to apply statistical reasoning. For this analysis to be valid, it is necessary to have enough data that the concepts of "confidence interval" and "hypothesis testing" are well defined for the quantities of interest—typically mean and standard deviation. In the case of single humped distributions, required sample size is proportional to the standard deviation of the data. Statistically stable practices have less variation than statistically unstable practices, so they require less data to reach valid conclusions. The exact number of data points depends on the specific distribution being used. Analyses that are free of distribution assumptions (non–parametric analysis) typically take more, not less data.

a performance problem. In contrast, it is reasonable to expect that a formal inspection of the design, a formal inspection of the code, and a formal performance test will all have a reproducible probability of discovering that same design defect, although the probabilities associated with each may differ.

> **Warning:** There may be simpler, more elegant proofs of the above results than what follows. If algebra or statistics give you a headache or other trauma, the author apologizes for any discomfort from what follows.

Analysis & Derivation

Suppose three or more adjacent quality practices that find and fix defects are performed in series, e.g., personal desk check, one-on-one peer review, compile and fix, formal inspection, unit testing, etc.[4] Also suppose the cost-effectiveness of each is measurable.[5] Please note that "cost" can be any independent variable of interest: dollars, labor hours, schedule impact, etc:

- Let Q_j be quality practice "j" where "j" is 1, 2, …
- Let F_j be the fixed and sunk costs of quality practice Q_j.[6] Presumably F_j will be small compared to other cost terms if there are a significant number of defects.
- Let C_j be the average cost per defect found and fixed for practice Q_j including verification practice V_j
- Let E_{Qj} be the average effectiveness – fraction of defects present found for

---

4   The case of three adjacent practices is sufficient. The general case can be derived using the same analytic approach, although with a bit more algebraic effort. Please note that if two adjacent quality practices find orthogonal sets of defects, then permuting them has no effect on overall cost-effectiveness.

5   Measurability of various things will depend on the process maturity of the organization. CMMI level 5 organizations will routinely address information needs related to process cost-effectiveness. CMMI level 1 organizations will be much less likely to be able to do so.

6   A fixed cost is one that does not grow in proportion to activity performed (see http://en.wikipedia.org/wiki/Fixed_cost). A sunk cost is one that has already been incurred and cannot be recovered to a significant degree (see http://en.wikipedia.org/wiki/Sunk_cost). Although they are quite different, those differences are not relevant to this analysis.

practice Q_j. Thus $E_j * C_j$ would be the probable cost of finding and fixing a defect with quality practice Q_j.

- Let E_{Vi} be the average effectiveness – fraction of defects present found for practice V_j. Thus $E_{Vj} * C_j$ would be the probable cost of finding and fixing a defect with quality practice V_j.
- Let I_{Rj} be the number of defects inserted by the rework due to Q_j.
- Let I_0 be the number of defects inserted by earlier development practices. There is no breakage in this analysis if we only consider defects that are discovered sometime in the product lifecycle. Defects that never get exercised have no cost impact.
- Let II_0 be the number of defects entering the second quality practice.
- Let III_{ij} be the number of defects escaping both when Q_i precedes Q_j.
- Let R_j be the rework activity associated with quality practice Q_j.
- Let V_j be the average effectiveness of the verification of rework performed in Q_j. For algebraic simplicity we will assume V_j is approximately equal to E_j.
- Let T_{LC} be the total lifecycle cost with subscripts indicating what quality practices are performed and in which order. Note that the letters "TLC" can also mean "Tender Loving Care" throughout the full lifecycle, which is what this author thinks is necessary to comply with the intent of section 804 of the Bob Stump Act of 2003.[7] Thus $T_{LC\ 12}$ refers to the case where Q_1 is performed before Q_2.
- Let T_{LC12} be the total lifecycle cost when both Q_1 and Q_2 are present.
- Let T_{LC1} be the total lifecycle cost when Q_1 is present and Q_2 is absent.
- Let T_{LC_2} be the total lifecycle cost when only Q_2 is present and Q_1 is absent.

Figure 2-1 shows the defect flow associated with quality practice Q_1. In Figure 2-1 the circles represent tasks, and the boxes represent collections of defects.

- Q_1 is a quality practice that finds a fraction E_{Q1} of the defects present in some set of work products.
- R_1 is the task that does the impact analysis and repair for each of the identified defects. This in principle may introduce a new set I_{R1} of defects.
- V_1 is the verification task that follows the rework effort. It verifies the solutions to the defects discovered in Q_1 and finds a fraction E_{V1} of the new defects.

---

7   *Bob Stump National Defense Authorization Act for Fiscal Year 2003*, Public Law No. 107-314, section 804, http://www.dod.mil/dodgc/olc/docs/2003NDAA.pdf (as of 9/13/2011).

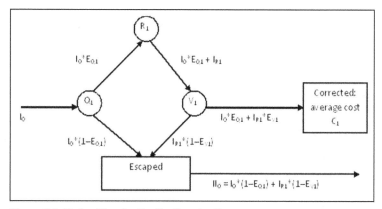

Figure 2-1. Defect Flow for Quality Practice Q_1

- Corrected defects do not propagate further.
- Escaped defects propagate to downstream processes.

When we stack two quality practices in a row, the input to the second practice consists of the escaped defects from the first practice. Algebraically this is accomplished by replicating figure one, changing the subscript 1 to 2 and replacing I_0 with $II_0 = I_0*(1-E_{QI}) + I_{RI}*(1-E_{VI})$ as is shown in Figure 2-2.

Given the model described by Figure 2-1 and Figure 2-2, it is now possible algebraically to answer a few questions:

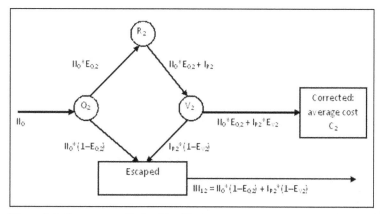

Figure 2-2. Downstream Defect Handling

1. What is the cost increase in reversing the order of application of the two practices, assuming all downstream defects eventually create an average cost C_3 per defect? [8]

$$
\begin{aligned}
T_{LC\ 12} ={}& F_1+C_1*(I_{R1}*E_{V1}+I_0*E_{Q1})+F_2+C_2*(I_{R2}*E_{V2}+II_0*E_{Q2})+F_3+C_3*III_{12} \\
={}& F_1+C_1*(I_{R1}*E_{V1}+I_0*E_{Q1})+F_2 \\
& +C_2*\{I_{R2}*E_{V2}+[I_0*(1-E_{Q1})+I_{R1}*(1-E_{V1})]*E_{Q2}\}+F_3+C_3*III_{12} \\
={}& F_1+F_2+F_3+C_1*I_{R1}*E_{V1}+C_2*I_{R2}*E_{V2}+C_1*I_0*E_{Q1} \\
& +C_2*I_0*(1-E_{Q1})*E_{Q2}+C_2*I_{R1}*(1-E_{V1})*E_{Q2}+C_3*III_{12}
\end{aligned}
$$

Equation 1

$$
\begin{aligned}
T_{LC\ 21} ={}& F_1+F_2+F_3+C_2*I_{R2}*E_{V2}\qquad +C_1*I_{R1}*E_{V1}+C_2*I_0*E_{Q2} \\
& +C_1*I_0*(1-E_{Q2})*E_{Q1}+C_1*I_{R2}*(1-E_{V2})*E_{Q1}+C_3*III_{21}
\end{aligned}
$$

Equation 2

and

$$
\begin{aligned}
III_{12} ={}& I_{R2}*(1-E_{V2})+II_0*(1-E_{Q2}) \\
={}& I_{R2}*(1-E_{V2})+[I_0*(1-E_{Q1})+I_{R1}*(1-E_{V1})]*(1-E_{Q2}) \\
III_{21} ={}& I_{R1}*(1-E_{V1})+[I_0*(1-E_{Q2})+I_{R2}*(1-E_{V2})]*(1-E_{Q1})
\end{aligned}
$$

so

$$
(III_{21}-III_{12}) = I_{R1}*E_{Q2}*(1-E_{V1})-I_{R2}*E_{Q1}*(1-E_{V2})
$$

thus

$$
(T_{LC\ 21}-T_{LC\ 12}) = I_0*(C_2*E_{Q2}-C_1*E_{Q1})+
$$

---

8   Please note that it can be a bit subtle to make an accurate estimate of the probable downstream cost of undiscovered defects. We can, however, put a lower bound on this by considering only those defects actually discovered later in the lifecycle. Given defect injection techniques, it is actually possible to get statistically valid estimates of the number of undiscovered defects. This technique is discussed thoroughly in H.D. Mills, "Statistical Validation of Computer Programs" in *Software Productivity*, Dover House Publishing, 1988, pp. 71–82.

$$I_0 * [C_1 * (1-E_{Q2}) * E_{Q1} - C_2 * (1-E_{Q1}) * E_{Q2}] +$$
$$C_1 * I_{R2} * (1-E_{V2}) * E_{Q1} - C_2 * I_{R1} * (1-E_{V1}) * E_{Q2} +$$
$$C_3 * (III_{21} - III_{12})$$

$$= I_0 * (C_2 - C_1) * E_{Q1} * E_{Q2} + C_1 * I_{R2} * (1-E_{V2}) * E_{Q1} -$$
$$C_2 * I_{R1} * (1-E_{V1}) * E_{Q2} + C_3 * (III_{21} - III_{12})$$

$$(T_{LC\ 21} - T_{LC\ 12}) = I_0 * (C_2 - C_1) * E_{Q1} * E_{Q2} + C_1 * I_{R2} * (1-E_{V2}) * E_{Q1} -$$
$$C_2 * I_{R1} * (1-E_{V1}) * E_{Q2} + C_3 *$$
$$[I_{R1} * E_{Q2} * (1-E_{V1}) - I_{R2} * E_{Q1} * (1-E_{V2})]$$

Dividing this equation by $C_3 * I_0 * E_{Q1} * E_{Q2}$ expresses this result in terms of dimensionless ratios:

$$(T_{LC\ 21} - T_{LC\ 12}) / C_3 * I_0 * E_{Q1} * E_{Q2} = 0$$

or

$$(C_2 - C_1) / C_3 + [(C_3 - C_2) / C_3] * (I_{R1} / I_0) * (1-E_{V1}) / E_{Q1} -$$
$$[(C_3 - C_1) / C_3] * (I_{R2} / I_0) * (1-E_{V2}) / E_{Q2} = 0$$

Equation 3

When the left-hand side is positive, it is more cost-effective to perform Q_1 before Q_2. The solution to this equation divides the parameter space into two regions—one in which the interchange is cost-effective and one in which it is not.

Although the first term is the one intuition would quickly identify, please note that because C_3 can be much larger than either C_1 or C_2, the second and third terms may dominate the outcome, especially during the Operations & Maintenance phase. Note that the fixed cost contributions all cancel exactly.

> **In general, the quality practices should be ordered by increasing average cost to find and fix defects. Fixed costs do not affect this conclusion, but significant differences either in defect detection effectiveness or in the effectiveness of verifying rework-induced defects can modify the conclusion.**

2. What is the cost of adding or dropping a quality practice?

A. Suppose we add or drop Q_1:

$$T_{LC\_12} = F_1 + F_2 \quad + C_1 * I_{R1} * E_{V1} \quad + C_2 * I_{R2} * E_{V2} + C_1 * I_0 * E_{Q1}$$
$$+ C_2 * I_0 * (1 - E_{Q1}) * E_{Q2} + C_2 * I_{R1} * (1 - E_{V1}) * E_{Q2} + F_3 + C_3 * III_{12}$$

where

$$III_{12} = I_{R2} * (1 - E_{V2}) + [I_0 * (1 - E_{Q1}) + I_{R1} * (1 - E_{V1})] * (1 - E_{Q2})$$

$$T_{LC\_2} = F_2 + C_2 * (I_{R2} * E_{V2} + I_0 * E_{Q2}) + F_3 + C_3 * III\_2$$

Equation 4

where

$$III\_2 = I_0 * (1 - E_{Q2}) + I_{R2} * (1 - E_{V2})$$

so

$$(III\_2 - III_{12}) = [I_0 * E_{Q1} - I_{R1} * (1 - E_{V1})] * (1 - E_{Q2})$$

thus

$$(T_{LC\_2} - T_{LC\_12}) = (I_0 * E_{Q1} + I_{R1} * E_{V1}) * (C_2 * E_{Q2} - C_1) +$$
$$C_3 * [I_0 * E_{Q1} - I_{R1} * (1 - E_{V1})] * (1 - E_{Q2}) - [F_1 + C_2 * I_{R1} * E_{Q2}]$$

Equation 5

This case will require individual analysis using actual (or accurately estimated) cost performance data.

Keeping/adding Q_1 is better if

$$(I_0 * E_{Q1} + I_{R1} * E_{V1}) * (C_2 * E_{Q2} - C_1) + C_3 * [I_0 * E_{Q1} - I_{R1} * (1 - E_{V1})] * (1 - E_{Q2})$$
$$> [F_1 + C_2 * I_{R1} * E_{Q2}]$$

Equation 6

Indeed, if C_3 is sufficiently large and I_{R1} is sufficiently small, it will always be practical to keep/add a quality practice. However, if I_{R1} is sufficiently large, then the converse will be true. In this case, the cost incurred due to mistakes inserted during rework swamps the value of mistakes actually found and fixed. Under those conditions it is better to drop the (broken) quality practice.

It is also true that very high fixed costs can cause a quality practice to become impractical. This is especially true when the "cost" of primary concern is a very aggressive development schedule commitment. It takes serious discipline on the part of both development management and customer management to put long-term goals before short-term concerns. Recent Congressional and Defense Department efforts to emphasize total lifecycle costs appears to be an attempt to provide a context in which this long term focus is even possible.[9]

B. Suppose we add or drop Q_2:

$$T_{LC1\_} = F_1 + C_1 * (I_{R1} * E_{V1} + I_0 * E_{Q1}) + F_3 + C_3 * III_{1\_}$$

$$T_{LC\ 12} = F_1 + C_1 * (I_{R1} * E_{V1} + I_0 * E_{Q1}) + F_2 + C_2 * (I_{R2} * E_{V2} + II_0 * E_{Q2}) + F_3 + C_3 * III_{12}$$

$$(T_{LC1\_} - T_{LC\ 12}) = C_3 * (III_{1\_} - III_{12}) - F_2 - C_2 * (I_{R2} * E_{V2} + II_0 * E_{Q2})$$

---

9   See for instance (current as of 2011):

• MIT, *Lean Advancement Initiative,* http://lean.mit.edu.

• T. McElroy, "Managing to the Acquisition Program Baseline," http://www.dau.mil/conferences/2005/Wednesday/B1-1345-McElroy-CR73.pdf.

• S.K. Fuller, "Guidance on Life-Cycle Cost Analysis Required by Executive Order 13123," April 2005, Department of Energy, Federal Energy Management Program, http://www1.eere.energy.gov/femp/pdfs/lcc_guide_05.pdf.

• Executive Orders 13101 and 13123, see http://www.archives.gov/federal-register/executive-orders/disposition.html (as of 10/10/2011).

• OMB Circular A-94, see http://www.whitehouse.gov/omb/circulars_a094/ (as of 10/10/2011).

• FAR Part 7.1, especially 7.105 and Part 52.248-2 (b) and 52.248-3, see https://www.acquisition.gov/far/97-05/pdf/07.pdf (as of 10/10/2011).

• "Life Cycle Cost Optimization" and "Affordability and Life-Cycle Resource Estimates," *Defense Acquisition Guidebook,* section 5.1.3.5 and chapter 3, respectively.

but $III_1 = II_0$, so

$$
\begin{aligned}
(T_{LC1} - T_{LC\,12}) &= C_3*\{II_0-[II_0*(1-E_{Q2})+I_{R2}*(1-E_{V2})]\} \\
&\quad - F_2 - C_2*(I_{R2}*E_{V2} + II_0*E_{Q2}) \\
&= C_3*\{II_0*E_{Q2}-I_{R2}*(1-E_{V2})]\}-C_2*(I_{R2}*E_{V2}+II_0*E_{Q2})-F_2 \\
&= (C_3-C_2)*II_0*E_{Q2}+(C_3-C_2)*E_{V2}*I_{R2}-F_2-C_3*I_{R2}
\end{aligned}
$$

We should retain/add Q_2 provided $(T_{LC1} - T_{LC\,12}) > 0$. This can be expressed as

$$(C_3-C_2)*II_0*E_{Q2}+(C_3-C_2)*E_{V2}*I_{R2}>F_2+C_3*I_{R2}$$

or

$$II_0*E_{Q2}+I_{R2}*E_{V2} > (C_3*I_{R2}+F_2)/(C_3-C_2)$$

Equation 7

Therefore, one should retain/add Q_2, provided the second practice fixes more defects during rework than the second practice creates during rework, and provided C_3 is much larger than either F_2 or C_2.

Worked Example

To make the results more solid, consider a software development effort delivering a million lines of code by a team of 100 software developers over 5 years. Given that software developers tend to change jobs quickly to keep their skills current, one can assume that defects found during design and coding will be fixed and verified by the original author and that defects found late in testing will be fixed and verified by someone other than the original author. Fixed and sunk costs will be ignored, and some average error rates and costs for this team of developers will be guessed:

- 20 defects per thousand lines of code inserted during coding and design: $I_0 = 20000$
- Inspection catches 3 out of every 4 defects present: $E_{Q1} = 0.75$
- 3 new defects are created for every 10 fixed: $I_{R1} = 0.3*0.75*20000 = 4500$ (please note this assumes I_{R1} is proportional to I_0)

- Defect detection and repair costs about 1 labor hour each: $C_1 = 1.0$
- Rework detection catches 9 out of 10 newly created defects: $E_{V1} = 0.9$
- Pre-delivery testing detects 6 defects out of 10 defects: $E_{Q2} = 0.6$
- Test rework inserts 5 new defects for every 10 fixed (not the original author): $I_{R2} = 1635$
- Test rework detection catches 6 out of 10 newly created defects (not the original rework verifier): $E_{V2} = 0.6$
- Test detection and repair costs 40 labor hours each: $C_2 = 40$
- Post-delivery error detection and repair costs 100 labor hours each: $C_3 = 100$
- Ignore fixed and sunk costs: $F_1 = F_2 = F_3 = 0$

In this case, spreadsheet analysis can be used to compute the various costs in labor hours:

- $T_{LC21} - T_{LC12} = 319022 > 0$ (don't permute the inspection and testing!)
- $T_{LC\_1} - T_{LC12} = 255060 > 0$ (don't drop the inspection)
- $T_{LC2\_} - T_{LC12} = 912150 > 0$ (don't drop the testing)

In this case, permuting the practices raises costs, as does dropping either practice.

Just for fun, it is now possible to guess at what happens when the two practices are inspection (Q_1) and unit test (Q_2). Which one should one go first? Assume unit tests are 90% effective at finding defects but take 4 hours each to find and fix the defect (additional unit tests get custom-built to diagnose and localize the defects), and verification finds 60% of defects created by the rework:

- $T_{LC21} - T_{LC12} = 319022 < 0$ (do the inspection first)
- $T_{LC\_1} - T_{LC12} = 565056 > 0$ (don't drop the inspection)
- $T_{LC2\_} - T_{LC12} = 402458 > 0$ (don't drop the testing)

This was assuming unit tests were 90% effective. One can ask at what unit test effectiveness the two practices are neutral to interchange—in this case, approximately 55%. In this case, if the unit tests are less than 55% effective at detecting defects, they should be performed prior to the inspection. *Please note: don't quote these example results! Please plug in your own measurements and get real answers to your questions.*

Indeed, if we use Equation 3, we can algebraically solve for interchange neutrality. On a diagram of the parameter space, the solution to this equation would divide the space into two regions: one in which the interchange is cost-effective and one in which it is not:

$$(C_2-C_1)/C_3 \quad +[(C_3-C_2)/C_3]*(I_{R1}/I_0)*(1-E_{V1})/E_{Q1}$$
$$-[(C_3-C_1)/C_3]*(I_{R2}/I_0)*(1-E_{V2})/E_{Q2} = 0$$

This can be solved for $1/E_{Q2}$ directly:

$$1/E_{Q2} = \{I_0/[(1-E_{V2})*I_{R2}]\}*[(C_2-C_1)/(C_3-C_1)+$$
$$[(C_3-C_2)/(C_3-C_1)]*(I_{R1}/I_0)*(1-E_{V1})/E_{Q1}]$$

Equation 8

---

provided the following inequality constraint holds:

$$0 < E_{Q2} <= 1$$

Conclusions

This analysis has demonstrated the following conclusions:

- In general, the quality practices should be ordered by increasing average cost to find and fix defects. Fixed costs do not affect this conclusion, but significant differences either in defect detection effectiveness or in the effectiveness of verifying rework induced defects can modify the conclusion.
- One should retain/add Q_2, provided the second practice fixes more defects during rework than the second practice creates during rework, and provided C_3 is much larger than either F_2 or C_2.

The Measurement and Traceability Challenge

Although the above analysis does not appeal to counterintuitive reasoning as is sometimes the case with statistical reasoning, there is a much more demanding barrier to benefiting from this analysis—getting organizations to track defects to their origin and to measure the associated costs of finding and fixing them. One problem is that quality practices are not always performed and measured the same way. Nor do they necessarily define or count defects in the same way. It is critical for an organization to establish a common set of definitions and standard measurements to avoid these issues.

To utilize the analysis presented here, each quality practice would need to measure the following items:

- C = the average cost to find and fix a defect discovered during the practice
- I_0 = the number of defects inserted prior to the practice
  - Either exclude those that are never found at all during the product lifecycle–they carry no actual cost, just potential cost,
  - or use a fault injection based experimental design to estimate I_0 with known accuracy.
- I_R = the number of defects inserted during rework resulting from the practice
- E_Q = the fraction of incoming defects (I_0) found by the quality practice
- E_V = the fraction of defects inserted during rework (I_R) found during verification

Even though there are only five items to measure, it is necessary that all quality practices use the same defect definition and that all[10] defects get traced to their point of insertion, preferably by an automated process. Effective version control and configuration management are essential here. Further, the variable cost, sunk cost, and fixed cost used in finding and fixing the defects would need to be captured.

---

10   If a program collects enough data and has a repeatable practice of using statistical techniques in process management, then "all" can be relaxed to the idea of a "statistically significant sample."

Chapter 3:
Code Inspections:
How Much Is Enough?

**How to Balance Work Product Inspection Cost
Against Testing Cost[1]**

G iven inspection effectiveness (defects found during inspection/ defects found during inspection plus those found during test) as a function of preparation rate (amount of work product examined per labor hour), it is then possible to construct a simple cost model that predicts

---

1   Adapted from "How Much Code Inspection is Enough?" *CrossTalk*, July 2001, http://www.crosstalkonline.org/storage/issue-archives/2001/200107/200107-McCann.pdf (as of 5/10/2011).

testing labor hours as a function of work product inspection preparation rate. This chapter develops that model and computes the optimum work product inspection preparation rate to minimize total cost (inspection + test). Existing program data (with significant caveats) have been used together with certain rough approximations to show that Fagan-style work product inspections obey a simple predictive cost model.

The purpose of this chapter is not to present actual performance data but to demonstrate how such data can be analyzed in the context of a cost model extending over multiple development processes—in this case, work product inspection, work product inspection rework, test, test rework, and regression testing. The purpose of the model is to demonstrate how to reduce development costs by managing how much time is spent preparing for work product inspections. All program data have been modified to protect the proprietary nature of that data. The conclusions and basic nature of the model are unaffected by these modifications.

This model can be used to optimize performance of future programs using a similar Fagan-style[2,3] work product inspection process with significant cost and schedule savings as well as quality improvement—in effect, better, faster, and cheaper. Such performance improvements should result in improvements in profitability, competitiveness, and customer confidence in both contract performance and product quality.

Further, the model is easily modified to work for other work products and cost drivers, e.g., design complexity. Given that work product inspection may not be particularly effective in finding design and requirements defects, it may make sense to extend the model to include more development processes, e.g., requirements development and requirements inspection, design development and design inspection, defect repair and associated inspection, etc.

Inspection, Test, and Accounting Processes

In order to perform this kind of analysis, it is necessary for a project to have defined, consistently executed processes that collect and retain sufficient data for work product inspection, work product inspection rework, testing, and testing rework. It is especially important in deriving this model that the

2   M.G. Fagan, "Design and Code Inspections to Reduce Errors in Program Development," *IBM Systems Journal*, vol. 15, no. 3, 1976.

3   M.G. Fagan, "Advances in Software Inspections," *IEEE Transactions on Software Engineering*, vol. SE-12, no. 7, July 1986.

inspection process was nearly statistically stable with respect to inspection preparation rate (lines of work product reviewed per labor hour). Otherwise, the statistical fits would have little predictive value. The cost data are also assumed available and traceable to these processes.

Inspection Effectiveness

It is not possible to know the true, exact percentage of work product defects found by work product inspections until all defects have been discovered, and that is not likely ever to happen in full. However, if it is assumed that essentially all work product defects found in testing could have been found in work product inspection, then there is value in studying the work product inspection effectiveness, the ratio of major work product inspection defects[4] divided by the sum of major work product inspection defects, plus the major work product defects found by testing. This ratio has the desirable property of ranging from 0 to 1 even though the relationship between major inspection defects and test defects is many-to-many rather than one-to-one. The model has the further benefit of quantifying how inspection preparation regulates testing costs.

When work product inspection effectiveness is averaged by Computer System Configuration Item (CSCI),[5] it is possible to develop a correlation between work product inspection preparation rate and work product inspection effectiveness. The correlation is well fit by a straight line with a y-intercept of 1.0 (see Fig. 3-1). The F-test[6] shows a confidence level in excess of 99% with the linear fit accounting for over 90% of the variation in the data. The F-test is a statistical test to verify that the function used to fit the data did not do so by accident.

Please note, however, that the fit function does not apply for very small

---

4   The Lockheed Martin Management & Data Systems definition of a major defect is a defect that will cause a malfunction or deviation from requirements or specifications, seriously violates policies or standards, indicates missing function, or makes the system unusable. The defect must be fixed, because it may cause some degree of project failure, economic loss, poor customer satisfaction, or contractual or legal breach.

5   A Computer Software Configuration Item (CSCI) is a large set of related functionality produced by one team of developers.

6   D.C. Montgomery and G.C. Runger, *Applied Statistics and Probability for Engineers*, John Wiley & Sons, Inc., 1994, pp. 315–317, 493–495, and 510–513. Also see the Microsoft Excel-97 SR-2 online help for the LINEST function, example 4, "Using the F and R2 Statistics."

preparation rates; at zero preparation rate, the preparation would never end. It is also not wise to extrapolate the fit function too far beyond the data on the right; generating a negative effectiveness is a clear indication of going too far.

The following variations to the data were performed and had only minor effects on the results (the slope changed by up to 10% and the goodness of fit parameters changed slightly):

- Restriction of inspection defects to major defects[7] rather than all defects found
- Removing any one of the data points
- Use of three separate selection criteria on the test defects
  - Total test defects
  - Work product-only test defects, including generated work product
  - Work product-only test defects, excluding generated work product.

In all of these cases, the effectiveness is well fit by a straight line that achieves 100% at zero preparation rate and declines by a constant amount for every 100 lines of work product per labor hour of inspection preparation review. See Figure 3-1.

Cost Model

The cost model should include all major costs that are affected by the inspection preparation rate. At the top level, this cost model includes the costs associated with just two development processes:

1. Work product inspections with inspection rework
2. Testing with test rework and regression testing.

A more detailed analysis including other work product development processes or including the effect of work product complexity on cost could not be supported due to absence of necessary data in the program databases. Work product complexity, both algorithmic complexity and interface complexity, would be expected to affect inspection effectiveness as well as

---

7   For a thorough discussion of world class quality and the cost of variation, see D.J. Wheeler and D.S. Chambers, *Understanding Statistical Process Control*, 2nd ed., SPC Press, 1992, pp. 141–147.

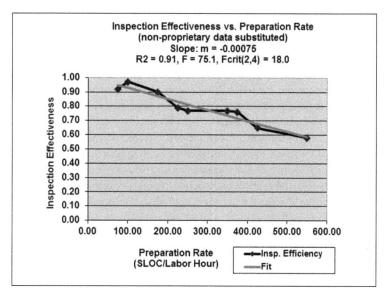

Figure 3-1. Least Squares Fit of Inspection Effectiveness to Preparation Rate

inspection rework labor hours and test rework labor hours, but these were excluded from this model due to the absence of appropriate supporting data.

In this model, total cost is the sum of the following items:

- work product inspection preparation labor,
- work product inspection meeting labor,
- work product inspection rework labor,
- the labor for running the full test suite once,
- testing rework labor,
- regression testing labor.

In deriving the cost function, the following statements are assumed to be approximately true:

- the inspection preparation labor is proportional to the amount of work product being reviewed
- the inspection meeting labor and the inspection rework labor are proportional to the number of major defects found in the inspections
- the test rework labor and the regression test labor are proportional to the number of major defects found during testing

Cost Function Derivation

Work product inspection labor consists of preparation labor, inspection meeting labor, and inspection defect rework labor. Preparation labor is just size divided by preparation rate, S/R. The inspection meeting labor is linearly related to the preparation labor because the meeting time will be driven by the number of candidate defects to be discussed and recorded. The sum of preparation labor and meeting labor is $C + D*S/R$, where C and D are the linear regression coefficients. Inspection rework is driven by the number of defects found, and that is the discoverable defect insertion rate "I" times the amount of work product inspected "S" times the inspection effectiveness "$(1 + m*R)$" times the labor to fix an average defect "W_{ri}."

Testing labor includes the cost of testing perfect work product "T_0*S" (running through the whole test suite once), rework-driven labor, and regression testing. Both regression testing and test rework will be driven by the number of defects detected during testing: the number escaping the inspections "$I*S*(-m)*R$" times the test effectiveness "E_t," times the labor for fixing and regression testing an average defect "T_r," Symbolically this can be expressed as follows:

$$T_c = T_0*S + C + D*S/R + W_{ri}*I*S*(1 + m*R) + T_r*E_t*I*S*(-m)*R$$

or

$$T_e = T_c - T_0*S = C + S*W_{ri}*I + S*D/R + S*I*(-m)*(T_r*E_t - W_{ri})*R$$

where

   C = y-intercept of empirical fit of total inspection labor (preparation plus meeting)

   D = slope of empirical fit of total inspection labor vs. preparation rate

   E_t = test effectiveness (defects found in test/defects found in test plus those found after test completion, excluding all defects that cannot be found by testing, e.g., requirements defects).

   I = discoverable work product defect rate = (work product inspection defect rate + test defect rate)

   m = slope of work product inspection effectiveness regression line

   R = work product inspection preparation rate (SLOC/labor hour)

   S = total SLOC inspected

SLOC = non-comment, non-blank, physical lines of work product. Any consistently used size measure will work, e.g., executable statements, function points, etc.

T_0 = labor for testing one line of perfect work product (regression testing not needed)

T_c = total cost (labor hours)

T_e = total excess cost due to discovered defects

T_r = labor per defect to do test rework and regression testing

W_{ri} = labor hours to rework a work product inspection defect

$C + D*S/R$ = labor for inspection preparation plus the inspection meeting

$I*S$ = defects present at work product inspection

$(1 + m*R)$ = work product inspection effectiveness

$I*S*(-m)*R$ = defects missed by the work product inspection that escape into test

$I*S*(1 + m*R)$ = defects found by the work product inspection

S/R = inspection preparation labor

T_0*S = total labor for testing perfect work product (regression testing not needed)

$T_r*E_t*I*S*(-m)*R$ = labor to do test rework

$W_{ri}*I*S*(1 + m*R)$ = labor for reworking defects found during the inspection

- a significant number of the major work product defects found by testing could have been found earlier in work product inspections

Using these assumptions, the total excess cost due to discovered defects can be expressed as follows:

$$T_e = C + S*W_{ri}*I + S*D/R + S*I*(-m)*(T_r*E_t - W_{ri})*R.$$

Equation 9

See the sidebar for the derivation of this cost function and for the definitions of the variables and terms.

Cost Optimization

The optimum work product inspection preparation rate is obtained by finding the point at which the cost function has a minimum. A minimum is found by setting the first derivative of the total cost with respect to work product inspection preparation rate equal to zero, solving for work product inspection preparation rate, and verifying that the point is a minimum and not a maximum or an inflection point:

$$I*S*(-m)*(T_r*E_t - W_{ri}) - D*S/R^2 = 0$$

The result is the following formula for the optimum preparation rate:

$$R_* = SQRT\{D/[I*(-m)*(T_r*E_t - W_{ri})]\}$$

Equation 10

For demonstration purposes, the following values are used:

D = 4

E_t = 1.0 approximately (a very high quality requirement: man rated or species rated).

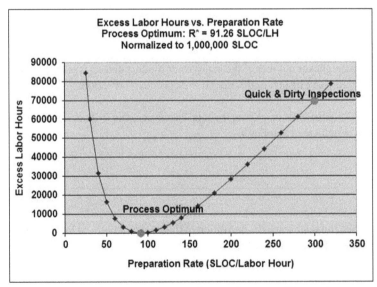

Figure 3-2. Murphy's Tongue—Excess Labor as a Function of Inspection Preparation Rate

I = 0.040 defects/SLOC

m = -0.00075 (SLOC/labor hour)$^{-1}$

S = 1,000,000 SLOC

T_r = 20 labor hours/defect

W_{ri} = 4 labor hours/defect

Substituting this demonstration data yields the following optimum work product inspection preparation rate:

$$R_* = 91.29 \text{ SLOC/labor hour.}$$

The relative cost in excess of the cost at the optimum rate is given by evaluating the difference in the total cost at a given rate minus the cost at the optimum rate:

$$T_M = S*D*(1/R - 1/R_*) + S*I*(-m)*(T_r*E_t - W_{ri})*(R - R_*)$$

Equation 11

Since this curve is shaped like a parabola that opens upward, there must be a unique preparation rate R_* that minimizes the total cost. See Figure 3-2, which is named in memory of Murphy's Law, because any variation from the optimum, no matter how well intentioned, will increase development costs.

The Cost of Variation

It is not enough to know the optimum preparation rate. No human process is without variation, so it is necessary to know the cost of variation. Whether a work product inspection is run slightly too fast or slightly too slow, the cost is higher than the minimum cost. This idea is summarized in the following definition: "world class quality is on target with minimum variance."[8]

The cost of variation is approximately parabolic with respect to deviations from the optimum preparation rate. Therefore the Taguchi cost of variance formula for this model is the averaged second derivative term in a Taylor expansion of the cost function:[9]

8   Ibid.
9   Ibid., pp. 143–147.

$$T_v = (D*S/ R_*^3)*<(R - R_*)^2>$$

Equation 12

where the angle brackets indicate computing the average over the whole dataset. Substituting example data yields

$$T_v = 5.26*<(R - R_*)^2> \text{ labor hours.}$$

This is an approximation of the exact cost behavior for this model, but it shows the salient point that variation itself has a cost that may be worth minimizing.

Conclusions

If a program collects the right data from the inspection, test, and cost accounting processes, performance and cost analysis can result in the ability to predict program cost and quality performance in terms of a single inspection process control: inspection preparation rate. With the right data, a second driver could be added to the model, e.g., work product complexity. This driver would be expected to affect inspection effectiveness as well as inspection rework labor hours and test rework labor hours.

Realistically, one ought to be able to achieve 90% work product inspection effectiveness by preparing at a cost-optimizing rate of about 100 SLOC/labor hour without any other change in the work product inspection process. To achieve further improvement—say, 99% effectiveness without increasing work product inspection cost—it would be necessary to improve the work product inspection process. There are several ways to do this:

- Use checklists that are improved each time they are used.
- Train each developer to develop and use an individualized checklist.
- Use Watts Humphrey's Team Software Process/Personal Software Process, which does both of the above and more.[10]

In conclusion, to get the best value from an inspection, it is more cost-effective to prepare for that inspection the way one would prepare for a final

---

10 W.S. Humphrey, M. Lovelace, and R. Hoppes, *Introduction to the Team Software Process,* Addison-Wesley, 1999.

In the example using the optimal 91.29 SLOC/labor hour preparation rate rather than a "quick and dirty" 300 SLOC/labor hour results in savings of nearly 70,000 labor hours/MSLOC (millions of dollars/MSLOC at any realistic labor rate). If the work product inspection process could be modified to be 99% efficient without increasing work product inspection costs, then the savings would potentially exceed 107,000 labor hours/MSLOC. Such potential improvement makes clear the value in performing work product inspections at a deliberate pace and reliably recording certain key information to enable optimization of program performance. With this kind of analysis and with reliably recorded data, **simultaneously working better, faster, and cheaper really is possible!**

exam in college: somewhere between reading the material as one would read a light novel for entertainment and preparing as thoroughly as one would for a PhD thesis defense.

Acknowledgments

The author would like to thank John Gibson of Lockheed Martin Mission Systems and Pat Dorazio, Earl Pape, and Bernie Pindell of Lockheed Martin Management & Data Systems, Gaithersburg, MD, for reading this report and making numerous helpful suggestions. Thanks are also due to Dr. Abol Ardalan of The University of Maryland University College for teaching me the value of cost models and how they are built and to Dr. Gary Kaskowitz of The University of Maryland University College for teaching me basic business statistics.

Chapter 4:
When Is It Cost-Effective to Use Formal Work Product Inspections?[1]

T he purpose of this chapter is to present a way to determine quantita-tively the parametric limits to cost-effectiveness of work product in-spections based on a previously published model. This analysis leads to the conclusion that it is cost-effective to inspect both original code and most modifications to the code after initial coding. Any exceptions should be carefully considered based on quantitative analysis of the projected impact of the exceptions. Further, any proposed substitution for rigorous inspec-

---

1   Adapted from "When is it Cost Effective to use Formal Software Inspec-tions?" *CrossTalk*, March 2004, http://www.crosstalkonline.org/storage/issue-archives/2004/200403/200403-McCann.pdf (as of 10/10/2011).

tions should be carefully evaluated for cost-effectiveness prior to replacing or modifying the process.

In this author's experience, the two following issues are discussed qualitatively when program management decides what to inspect and what data to collect:

- Deciding whether or not to inspect work products based on a qualitative understanding of various limiting parameters such as work product size, preparation rate, or expected defect density.
- Deciding whether or not to collect and analyze inspection data based on a qualitative understanding of the return on investment (ROI) on collecting, analyzing, and using inspection metrics.

This chapter improves on this practice by estimating quantitatively, from the perspective of an existing quantitative cost model [1], both the parametric boundaries of inspection cost-effectiveness and ROI for collecting and analyzing inspection metrics.

It is important to note that there are several different budgetary strategies that may be applied when making process implementation choices. Here are three examples ordered from long-term to short-term in the planning horizon:

- Minimize total cost of ownership, including post-delivery maintenance costs.
- Minimize overall development cost excluding post-delivery maintenance costs.
- Assure that inspection overhead costs are exactly balanced by reductions in test rework costs (this does not minimize costs).

These goals may be examined within the context of the existing quantitative cost model. Then, once the inspection process is quantitatively managed, it becomes possible to study the value of various emerging best practices in inspections (see Appendix A).

Although other process models and cost-effectiveness analyses are possible, the results are similar [2, 3]. It is possible and reasonable quantitatively to analyze the cost-effectiveness of inspections with respect to the model parameters.

The Cost Model

If sufficient metrics are collected during a development project, it is possible to know the cost structure of the various development processes. That in turn enables modeling of the cost impact of all processes that discover work product defects. In particular, Chapter 3: "Code Inspections: How Much is Enough?" focuses on modeling of the impact of work product inspections on the overall cost of systems development [1]. This is an example of how you might model the impact of all quality practices that detect defects. All such practices are data-linked to testing via the defects that escape into the test phase. Indeed, you could use the code inspection cost function directly on other work products with only minor reassignment of the meanings of the cost parameters; just compare the cost of finding and fixing a defect with an inspection to the cost of finding and fixing that same defect by another means later in the development lifecycle.

A central result of Chapter 3 is the total cost function for work product inspections plus work product testing. For this purpose all regression testing and rework of test defects were lumped into a single term. That cost function follows:

```
(total cost) = (inspection fixed cost) + (regression fixed
                         cost)

         + (inspection preparation plus meeting cost)

         + (inspection rework cost)

         + (test rework cost plus regression cost)
```

or

$$T_c = C_i + C_r + D*S/R + W_{ri}*I*S*[1-(-m)*R] + T_r*E_r*I*S*(-m)*R$$

Equation 13

Note: m<0, so (-m)>0 (see the sidebar on "Symbol Definitions").

This formula includes two terms derived from regression analysis of inspection data. The first such term, $D*S/R$, combines the inspection preparation labor with the meeting labor because they were found to be co-linear. D is the regression coefficient, and S/R is the preparation labor per inspection (code size S divided by the preparation rate R). The second term includes the linear regression model for inspection effectiveness as a function of preparation rate, $W_{ri}*I*S*[1-(-m)*R]$, where W_{ri} is the average cost of fixing a defect

Symbol Definitions

Please note that subscripts indicate the following:

i refers to inspections.

r refers to rework after testing.

ri refers to rework after inspection.

R refers to regression testing and fixing after delivery.

C_i = Y-intercept of empirical fit of total inspection labor (preparation plus meeting), overhead cost per inspection (labor hours).

C_r = Testing cost overhead per regression test suite, overhead cost per set of test defects (test overhead costs prevented by an inspection) (labor hours).

C_R = Testing cost overhead per regression test suite, overhead cost per set of test defects found by the customer (test overhead costs prevented by an inspection) (labor hours).

D = Slope of empirical fit of inspection labor plus meeting labor vs. preparation labor (dimensionless ratio).

E_r = Test effectiveness (defects found in test/defects found in test plus those found after test completion, excluding all defects that cannot be found by testing, e.g., requirements defects when the tests are required to be consistent with documented requirements and the testers are not allowed to challenge the validity of the requirements) (% defects found in this phase).

E_R = Customer test effectiveness (defects found in acceptance test plus those found in user operation/those defects plus estimated remaining defects) (% defects found by the customer).

I = Discoverable code defect rate = (code inspection defect rate + test defect rate) (defects/SLOC).

LH = Labor Hours (this is much easier to record and to use than monetary cost).

m = Slope of code inspection effectiveness regression line (%/(SLOC/LH)).

R = Code inspection preparation rate (SLOC/labor hour).

R* = The cost-optimizing code inspection preparation rate (SLOC/labor hour).

S = Total SLOC inspected.

SLOC = Non-comment, non-blank, physical lines of code. Any consistently used size measure will work, e.g., executable statements, function points, etc.

T_0 = Labor for testing perfect code (regression testing not needed) (labor hours).

T_c = Total cost (labor hours).

T_M = Total excess cost due to non-optimal inspection preparation (labor hours).

T_r = Labor per defect to do test rework and regression testing (labor hours/defect).

T_R = Labor per defect to do rework and regression testing of defects found by the customer and user community (labor hours/defect).

W_{ri} = Labor hours to rework a code inspection defect (labor hours/defect).

found in an inspection, I is the density of defects found by all means (this increases linearly throughout the lifecycle), and m is the linear regression co-efficient relating inspection preparation rate and effectiveness (the fraction of discovered defects found by inspection).

The last term models the testing cost due to defects that escaped into the test process because they were missed by the inspection, $T_r*E_r*I*S*(-m)*R$, where T_r is the average cost of finding and fixing one defect in testing, E_r is the effectiveness of the testing process at discovering defects, and $I*S*(-m)*R$ is the number of (eventually) discovered defects not found by work product inspection.

Method

For each model parameter there may be a corresponding boundary value that distinguishes a process operation that is cost-effective from one that is not. In each case, you compare the inspection costs with the test costs that may be prevented by conducting inspections. When the benefit exceeds the cost, it is cost-effective to conduct inspections. You may calculate the ROI by subtracting the cost from the benefit and dividing the result by the cost. Positive ROI justifies conducting inspections.

The original model is based on analysis of inspection, test, and cost data for a proprietary project at Lockheed Martin Management and Data Systems. The data used in this paper are simulated data having the same

Term Definitions

Ci+D*S/R = Labor for inspection preparation plus the inspection meeting.

I*S = Defects present at code inspection.

(1+m*R) = Code inspection effectiveness.

I*S*(-m)*R = Defects missed by the code inspection that escape into test.

I*S*(1+m*R) = Defects found by the code inspection.

S/R = Inspection preparation labor.

T0*S= Total labor for testing perfect code (regression testing not needed).

Tr*Er*I*S*(-m)*R = Labor to do test rework.

TR*ER*(1-Er)*I*S*(-m)*R = Labor to fix defects found after delivery to the customer.

Wri*I*S*(1+m*R) = Labor for reworking defects found during the inspection.

characteristics as the real data; this substitution is required to protect the proprietary nature of the original program data and does not change the conclusions that flow from the model analysis.

Results

The cost model is reviewed and extended to include post-delivery marginal maintenance costs. Then a cost-effectiveness model is developed and applied to several process model parameters: inspection preparation rate, inspection package size, defect insertion density, the significance of inspection effectiveness correlation, and the ratio of total effort to preparation effort. The model produces a simple inequality that, if true, predicts inspections to be cost-effective.

Cost Minimization

Once the decision has been made to inspect a work product, that inspection should be managed so that it minimizes the total applicable cost function. If regression testing is not 100 percent effective, and minimizing the total cost of ownership is the goal, then Equation 13 needs cost terms to model the cost of fixing defects found after delivery to the customer: $C_R + T_R*E_R*(1-$

$E_r)*I*S*(-m)*R$ where it is expected that $T_R > T_r$. This results in a linear interpolation of the probable costs in testing and customer use:

$$T_c = C_i+C_r+C_R+D*S/R+W_{ri}*I*S*[1-(-m)*R]+T_{eff}*I*S*(-m)*R$$

Equation 14

where

$$T_{eff} = [T_r*E_r+T_R*E_R*(1-E_r)].$$

In either case, the same mathematical procedure is used to find parameter values that minimize the cost function.

Preparation rate is the only model parameter that causes the cost function to achieve a cost minimum, and it does so in the region of applicability of the linear regression fit for inspection effectiveness. This regression fit model is thus bounded between zero and one (100 percent effective inspections):

$$0 <= [1-(-m)*R] <= 1.$$

Substituting the model data from a previous article [1] gives:

$$0 < R <= 1/(-m) = 1/0.00075=1329 \text{ SLOC/Labor Hour (LH)}.$$

If the preparation rate approaches either boundary, a non-linear regression model will be more appropriate, provided sufficient data exist to validate the model.

Product size S and defect insertion rate I both have a positive slope in the cost function (the slopes are given by derivatives with respect to model parameters):

$$dT_c/dS = D/R+W_{ri}*I*[1-(-m)*R]+T_{eff}*I*(-m)*R > 0$$

and

$$dT_c/dI = W_{ri}*S*[1-(-m)*R]+T_{eff}*S*(-m)*R > 0.$$

Clearly, both S and I drive up costs linearly, so any scheme that reduces either total size or defect insertion rate will drive down development costs, provided size and defect insertion rate are independent—more about that later.

The effect of the slope of the regression fit m is determined by the relative effect of the cost of finding and fixing defects at various points in the development lifecycle:

$$dT_c/d(-m) = T*I*S*R > 0$$

where

$$T = (T_{eff}-W_{ri}).$$

It is expected that this will be strongly positive. Therefore, any process change that improves the effectiveness of finding defects at higher preparation rates will reduce costs. For instance, automating some of the checks in the inspection process reduces the labor spent finding those classes of defects.

The minimum process cost occurs at a preparation rate for which the slope of the cost function is zero. Thus the cost optimizing preparation rate is found by setting to zero the first derivative of the cost function with respect to preparation rate:

$$dT_c/dR = -D*S/R^2+T*I*S*(-m) = 0$$

$$R^* = \sqrt{D/[T*I*(-m)]}$$

Equation 15

where

$$T = (T_{eff}-W_{ri})$$

and

$$T_{eff} = [T_r*E_r+T_R*E_R*(1-E_r)].$$

Cost-Effectiveness

With a cost-effectiveness strategy, it is necessary to derive an expression that shows how inspections can be expected to pay for their own overhead, assuming, on average, that they will be conducted at the cost-optimizing preparation rate. For this example, the cost of finding and fixing defects found by the customer is not included. This expression can be derived by comparing the average cost of finding a defect in an inspection with the associated cost savings in reduced test rework and regression testing. The cost payback is given by the following condition:

```
(Inspection Costs) <= (Regression Test and Rework Costs
                  Prevented)
```

or

$$C_i+D*S/R+W_{ri}*I*S*[1-(-m)*R] \;<=\; C_r/N+T_r*E_r*I*S*[1-(-m)*R]$$

Equation 16

or, presuming the inspections will be conducted at the optimum preparation rate,

$$(C_i-C_r/N)+D*S/R^* \;<=\; (T_r*E_r-W_{ri})*I*S*[1-(-m)*R^*].$$

Equation 17

The right hand side of Equation 17 is the average test rework cost per defect prevented, minus the average inspection rework cost per defect found, times the number of defects found by the inspection, $I*S*[1-(-m)*R^*]$. C_i is the average overhead cost per inspection, C_r is the average overhead cost per test rework and regression test cycle, and N is the average number of inspections bundled per regression cycle. Given equations (16) and (17), it is now possible to investigate the parametric boundaries or clip levels of cost-effectiveness with respect to the cost model parameters: preparation rate, inspection size, defect injection rate, repair costs, and inspection effectiveness regression coefficient. By making the following substitutions:

$C = C_r/N- C_i$	(net average fixed costs)
N	(average inspections per regression suite)
$T = T_r*E_r - W_{ri}$	(net average repair costs)
$R^* = \sqrt{D/[I*(-m)*T]}$	(optimum preparation rate)
$X = \sqrt{D*(-m)}$	(regression coefficients)
$Y = \sqrt{I*T}$	(Y^2 is the net burden rate for missed defects)

the governing relationship, Equation 17, for the limits of cost-effective operation may be simplified:

$$2*X \;<=\; Y + C/(S*Y).$$

Equation 18

The following sections will explore the implications of this model for each of the model parameters.

Cost Balancing Preparation Rate

Solving Equation 16 for R gives the preparation rate that assures payback of overhead costs in reduced regression testing and rework prior to delivery to the customer:

$$D*S-[C+T*I*S]*R+T*I*S*(-m)*R^2 \:<= \:0$$

Equation 19

where it is expected that $T=(T_r*E_r - W_{ri})>0$ and $C=(C_r-C_i)>0$. This is of the form $a*R^2 + b*R + c <= 0$, which has two bounding roots (small and large):

$$R_S = -2*c*sign(b)/(|b|+\sqrt{b^2-4*a*c})$$

and

$$R_L = -sign(b)*(|b|+\sqrt{b^2-4*a*c})/(2*a)$$

where

$$a = T*I*S*(-m)$$
$$b = -[C + T*I*S]$$
$$c = D*S$$

Any preparation rate between these two roots will yield cost-effective inspections:

$$R_s \:<= \:R \:<= \:R_L.$$

The condition for real valued solutions is that $(b2 – 4*a*c) >= 0$. The two real roots will bound the region of interest – the left-hand side of Equation 19 is negative. Using the data from [1] and finding Ci as the y-intercept for small inspections [1]:

$$C_r =0, \:C_i =2, \:m= -0.00075, \:I=0.040, \:T_r = 20, \:W_{ri} =4, \:D=4,$$
$$S=200$$

and assuming $E_r = 1.0$ gives $R_S = 6.38$ SLOC/Labor Hour (LH), and $R_L = 1306$ SLOC/LH.

By comparison, the cost-optimizing preparation rate 91.29 SLOC/LH is equal to the geometric mean of the bounding values:

$$R^* = \sqrt{R_S*R_L}$$
$$= \sqrt{c/a}$$
$$= \sqrt{D/[T*I*(-m)]}$$

The preparation rate that provides the most negative value for Equation 19 is found by setting the first derivative of Equation 19 with respect to R equal to zero:

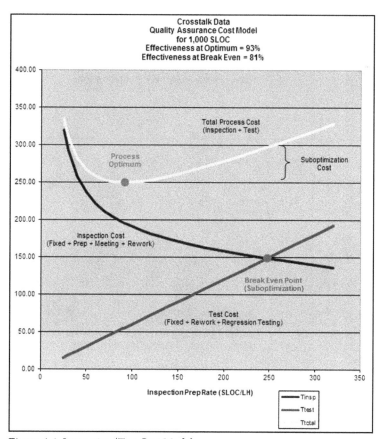

Figure 4-1. Inspection/Test Cost Model

$$-(C + T*I*S) + 2*T*I*S*(-m)*R = 0$$

or

$$R_p = (C + T*I*S)/[2*T*I*S*(-m)].$$

Using the above parameters, R_p = 656 SLOC/LH, which is well below $1/(-m)$ = 1329 SLOC/LH for regression model validity but well above the overall cost-optimizing value 91.29 SLOC/LH. Please note: if $C_i = C_r$ then $R_p = 1/(-2*m)$ = 664.5 SLOC/LH, which is the exact center of the region of applicability of the linear regression model.

While the parametric analysis of the cost-effectiveness strategy establishes the existence of cost-effectiveness boundaries for the inspection process, optimum cost performance is not obtained on the boundaries. Rather, the most cost-effective operation for the process is obtained when the optimum preparation rate is used. Figure 4-1 demonstrates this recommended practice.

It is worth noting that the inverse of the Total Process Cost function in Figure 4-1 is the test phase productivity. Figure 4-2 displays this function and demonstrates the effectiveness of inspections in controlling test phase productivity.

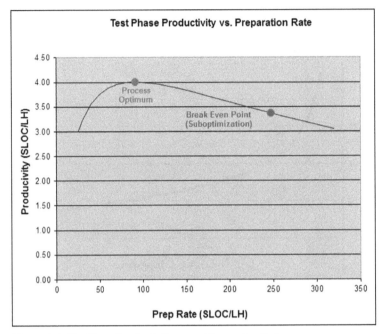

Figure 4-2. Test Phase Productivity versus Preparation Rate

The Smallest Size for a Cost-Effective Inspection

Solving Equation 18 for equality gives:

$$S_c = C/[\ Y*|2*X-Y|\ ]$$

Equation 20

where $S<=S_c$ when $2*X>Y$ and $S>=-S_c$ when $2*X<Y$.

Please note that there are two singularities: $2*X=Y$, where the net probable marginal rework costs equals twice the sum of meeting plus preparation costs; and $Y=0$, where inspection rework costs equal marginal regression testing and rework costs. Using the above data:

$$C_r=0,\ C_i=2,\ m=-0.00075,\ I=0.040,\ T_r=20,\ W_{ri}=4,\ D=4,$$
$$S=200$$

and assuming $E_r = 1.0$, using the cost optimizing preparation rate $R*=91.29$ SLOC/LH gives a constraint on size:

$$S >= S_c = 3.62\ SLOC.$$

That assumes the testing costs through System Level Test (SLT). Including the costs of Operation Release Level (ORL) testing increases the costs significantly to, say, approximately $T_r = 40$ and changes the cutoff:

```
S  = 1.53 SLOC.
 c
```

Please note that both values are very small. Very few defect fixes affect so little code. Indeed, if testing fixed costs exceed inspection fixed costs (for the same amount of code), $C_t/N > C_i$, and marginal testing costs prevented exceeds twice the marginal inspection cost incurred, $Y > 2*X$, then $-S_c < 0 < S$, and all code inspection sizes are cost-effective!

Defect Density Clip Level

Beginning with Equation 18

```
2*X <= Y + C/(S*Y)
```

and solving for Y gives two bounding conditions:

and

$$Y_S = (C/S)/[X + \sqrt{X^2 - C/S}\,]$$

$$Y = \sqrt{T*I} > Y_L = X + \sqrt{X^2 - C/S} > Y_S$$

Equation 21

Using the above simulated project data and the cost-optimizing preparation rate gives:

$$I >= \{\,[\,\sqrt{0.003} + \sqrt{0.003 + 2/S}\,\,]/\sqrt{T}\,\}^2$$

where $T = 16$ (SLT costs) or 36 (ORL costs).

Figure 4-3 shows that the defect insertion rate clip level increases for smaller code packages. It is important to know that defect insertion rates increase for smaller packages. Indeed, as demonstrated by Figure 4-2, the defect rate increases as the size decreases.[2] This is data from the Space Telescope Grant Management System (STGMS), which is a large Java applica-

---

2   By permission of Thomas Comeau, manager, Space Telescope Grant Management System (STGMS) project. Revision rate is the number of changes per file and is assumed to be representative of the defect rate.

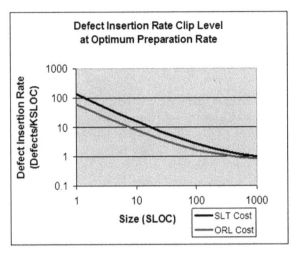

Figure 4-3. Defect Insertion Rate Clip Level versus Optimum Preparation Rate

tion of over 200,000 non-commented source statements. In the chart, *LN* is the natural logarithm.

This trend is not unique. The same trend may be seen on Figure 4-4, the public domain Jetty project (a Java server written in Java).[3] One might hypothesize that the slope of the regression line is explained by the observation that large classes get edited more often than small ones, and each editing session affords opportunity to review all that has been coded to date. In that case the effectiveness of defect detection by the author would be proportional to the number of opportunities to review the modules in the class. The total number of review opportunities (and the effort to build the class) would scale as the square of the number of modules. Hence the defect density would be roughly proportional to

$$1/\sqrt{Size}$$

if the modules are of similar size and complexity. The variance in the scaling would be sensitive to the variation in the review habits of the individual developers. As such, both defect detection and defect prevention would be

3   The data may be found at < http://sourceforge.net/cvs/?group_id=7322 >. The defect density data are not available. It is assumed that the revision density (revisions per file) will have the same character as defect density.

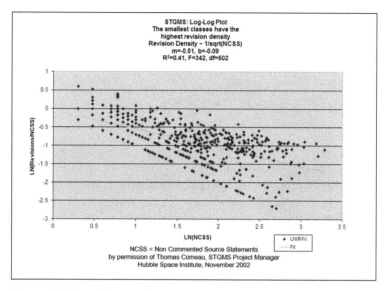

Figure 4-4. Space Telescope Grant Management System Revision Density Plot

subject to potential process improvement and training. In the chart, *LN* is the natural logarithm.

A further consideration is that reworked code is known to have a significantly higher defect insertion rate than initially written code, especially if the maintainer is not the original author. From Capers Jones [4], out of a total average defect load of five defects per function point, 0.4 defects/Function Point is contributed from bad fixes. That says that there is about an 8 percent probability of making a bad fix. That is a defect insertion rate of 80 defects/thousand single lines of code (KSLOC) in code repairs. This is significantly higher than the defect rate for new code that Capers Jones lists as 50 defects/KSLOC. From these charts it is very clear that inspections are justified for even small changes unless the regression cost is very low indeed. Post-delivery, the regression costs tend to be even greater, making the case even stronger for inspections.

Clip Level for Net Cost to Fix

One can also solve Equation 21 for the net cost to fix a defect:

$$Y = \sqrt{T*I} > Y_L = X + \sqrt{X^2 - C/S}$$

thus

$$T >= \{[X + \sqrt{X^2 - C/S}\,]\}^2/I.$$

Equation 22

Using the example data generates Figure 4-5.

Just as with defect density, one can solve Equation 18 for the critical linear regression coefficient *(-m)* above which inspection costs dominate regression test costs at the optimum preparation rate:

$$2*\sqrt{D*(-m)} = 2*X <= Y + C/(S*Y).$$

Solving for *(-m)* yields

$$(-m) <= (-m_c) = [Y + C/(S*Y)]^2/(4*D)$$

Equation 23

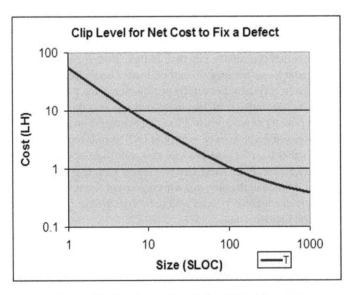

Figure 4-5. Clip Level for Net Cost to Fix a Defect Critical Regression Coefficient

Using the simulated program data gives the following figure:

$$(-m_c) = 0.0189 \text{ for } S=10 \text{ (small changes)}.$$

In the example data $(-m)$ = 0.00075, which is much less than the critical value. So, inspections are well justified even for small changes. However, there is a size cutoff that causes the numerator of Equation 23 to become zero:

$$S_c = -C/Y^2$$

$$S_c = 3.1 \text{ (SLT costs)}$$

or

$$S_c = 1.4 \text{ (ORL costs)}.$$

Please note that $(-m)$ must also be statistically distinct from zero at some acceptable confidence level, say $\alpha/2=0.025$ for a two-tail t-test. For this example, the standard error in $(-m)$ is 0.0000387, and *t-critical* is 2.3646. The minimum significant value for $(-m)$ is 2.3646*0.0000387=0.0000915, well below the actual value.

Critical Meeting Rate

By rearranging Equation 23 it is possible to specify the meeting rate above that it is not cost-effective to conduct inspection meetings:

$$D <= D_c = [Y + C/(S*Y)]^2/[4*(-m)].$$

Equation 24

For the example data, D_c = 101 for S = 10 and SLT costs and D_c = 356 for ORL costs. These are well above the example value D = 4, so time spent in the meeting does not constrain the cost- effectiveness of the process.

Return on Investment for Metrics Analysis— Knowing the Optimum Preparation Rate

First calculate *Total Process Cost* less *Cost at Optimum* evaluated at the unmanaged preparation rate:

$$T_M = S*D*(1/R - 1/R^*) + S*I*(-m)*T*(R - R^*).$$

Given the simulated data

```
C_r =0,  C_i =2,  m= -0.00075,  I=0.040,  T_r = 20,  W_ri =4,  D=4
```

with project teams averaging approximately $S = 600$ SLOC at $R = 300$ SLOC/LH, and $R^* = 91.29$ SLOC/LH, the excess process labor at the unmanaged preparation rate is

$$T_M = 41.8 \text{ LH/inspection.}$$

So, on average, using the overhead cost of setting up, managing, recording, and analyzing an average inspection (assuming a fair amount of automation and tool support), $C_i = 2$ LH, the ROI for collecting and analyzing metrics for an average inspection is substantial:[4]

$$\text{ROI} = (T_M - C)/C = (41.8-2)/2$$
$$\text{ROI} = 20.$$

In this case, on average, every hour spent collecting, recording, and analyzing inspection metrics will potentially return about 20 hours in reduced testing and fixing cost. The ROI will be even higher if one includes the added benefits of using the metrics to support defect causal analysis and associated process improvement to prevent future defects of a similar type from occurring [5, 6]. Clearly, it is critical to collect and analyze the inspection data and to manage the preparation rate accordingly.

Discussion and Recommendations

Within the context of the existing cost model, one can answer the initial question in the title of this chapter. The parametric boundaries of cost-effective operation have been derived and shown to impose relatively benign operational constraints. Further, it has been demonstrated that the return

---

4   This is the ROI just for the metrics collection and analysis using the simulated data. The ROI for the whole process will be different. For instance, see any of the following:

• D. O'Neil, "Setting Up a Software Inspection Program," *CrossTalk*, Feb. 1997.

• T. Gilb, "Optimizing Software Inspections," *CrossTalk*, Mar. 1998, http://www. crosstalkonline.org/storage/issue-archives/1998/199803/199803-Gilb.pdf.

• D. O'Neil, "National Software Quality Experiment: A Lesson in Measurement: 1992–1997," *CrossTalk*, Dec. 1998, p. 29, http://www.crosstalkonline.org/storage/issue-archives/1998/199812/199812-0-Issue.pdf.

on investment for collecting and analyzing inspection metrics well justifies doing so.

It is well known that the cost of finding and fixing defects increases throughout the development lifecycle. Since code is the last development phase prior to testing, since the cost to fix artifacts increases throughout the development lifecycle [7], and since it is reasonable that the cost to fix a test script would be similar to the cost to fix a code defect, it is therefore clear that earlier work products are even more cost-effective to inspect than code.

Therefore, because it is cost-effective to do so, it is established that performing rigorous inspections should be the default behavior for all work products that affect the quality of the delivered product, provided there is a documented development process with defined work products in addition to code. It is expected that any organization with an ISO-9001 certification or a rating above Capability Maturity Modelâ Integration Level 2 would have documented development processes and defined work products that affect the quality of delivered code.

Exceptions to this rule should be granted only after careful quantitative analysis of the cost impact of such exceptions using Equation 19 and Equation 22:

$$R^* = \sqrt{D/[I*(-m)*T]}$$
$$2*X <= Y + C/(S*Y).$$

where

$X = \sqrt{D*(-m)}$	(regression coefficients)
$C = (C_r + C_R)/N - C_i$	(net average fixed costs)
N	(average inspections per regression suite)
$T = T_r*E_r + T_R*E_R*(1-E_t) - W_{ri}$	(total net average marginal repair costs)
$Y = \sqrt{T*I}$	(Y^2 is the net burden rate for missed defects)
S	(size of inspected product – SLOC, etc.)

Given that inspections are run at (or near) the optimum preparation rate, then the model makes predictions about average achievable inspection effectiveness:

$$E^* = 1 - X/Y$$

Equation 25

and average test phase productivity:

$$P_r^* = S/T_c = 1/\{ [(C_r + C_R)/N + C_i]/S + I*W_{ri} + 2*X*Y \}.$$

Equation 26

Finally, it is recommended that any proposed substitution for formal inspections should be carefully evaluated for cost-effectiveness prior to replacing or modifying the existing process by deriving an equivalent cost model and performing equivalent analysis.

Acknowledgements

The author would like to thank Thomas Comeau, manager of the STGMS project, for providing the software defect data for the Space Telescope Grant Management System and for finding and making available the equivalent data from the Jetty project. Special thanks are due John Gibson of Lockheed Martin Mission Systems for his many reviews and improvement suggestions for this article. Thanks also go to Dr. Louis Blazy of The University of Maryland University College for his review and improvement suggestions. Further special thanks go to Dr. Michael A. Spencer for detailed composition review and resulting suggestions to improve both clarity and impact.

Appendix A

Even though the practice has existed since the mid 1970s, performing rigorous software inspections (at all) has been and continues to be an industry best practice [8]. Nevertheless, software inspections have room for improvement. Radice claims that 100 percent effective inspections are becoming more common and may someday become much more so [9, 10].[5] There are several best practices that may make significant contributions to that quest [11]:

- Use of a Quantitative Cost Model to manage the inspection process.
- Managing the inspection process via statistical process control (SPC) on preparation rate.
- Using a defect prevention process in conjunction with inspections to improve both product and process (check lists, tools, etc.).
- Use of SPC on both the preparation rate and the defect rate to trigger use of the defect prevention process [12].
- Use of Tools to automate parts of the inspection.
- Use of Perspective-Based Reading techniques to improve the effectiveness of the inspections [13].
- Use of pilot studies to measure the effect of proposed process improvements.
- Use of experimental design techniques to improve the cost-effectiveness of pilot studies of proposed process improvements.
- Given a validated model for the cost-effectiveness of inspections, it is possible to compare the regression line for cost-effectiveness of proposed variations to the regression line for the cost-effectiveness of the initial process. Standard statistical tests at a predetermined confidence level can then be applied to the difference, thus creating an objective standard for determining the cost-effectiveness of the process variation.

5   The company that has achieved repeatable 100 percent effective inspections is TATA Consultancy of India.

References

1. R.T. McCann, "How Much Code Inspection is Enough?" *CrossTalk*, July 2001, http://www.crosstalkonline.org/storage/issue-archives/2001/200107/200107-McCann.pdf.

2. K.A. Paton, "Cost-Effectiveness of Manual Code Inspection." *Proc. of the 11th International Workshop on Software Measurement*, Montreal, Aug. 2001.

3. K.A. Paton, "Should You Test the Code Before You Test the Program?" *Proc. of ESCOM 2001*, London, April 2001.

4. C. Jones, "Software Cost Estimation in 2002," Table 3, *CrossTalk*, June 2002, http://www.crosstalkonline.org/storage/issue-archives/2002/200206/200206-Jones.pdf.

5. R.G. Mays, C.L. Jones, G.J. Holloway, and D.P. Studinski, "Experiences with Defect Prevention," *IBM Systems Journal*, vol. 29, no. 1, 1990.

6. J.L. Gale, J.R. Tirso, and C.A. Burchfield, "Implementing the Defect Prevention Process in the MVS Interactive programming organization," *IBM Systems Journal*, vol. 29, no. 1, 1990.

7. B.W. Boehm, *Software Engineering Economics*, Prentice-Hall, 1981, p. 40, fig. 4-2.

8. R.L. Glass, "Inspections—Some Surprising Findings," *Communications of the ACM*, vol. 42, no. 4, Apr. 1999, pp. 17–19.

9. R. Radice, *High Quality Low Cost Software Inspections*. Paradoxicon Publishing, 2002, pp. 14-402–14-403.

10. R. Radice et al., "One on One Inspections." *Proc. 2001 Software Technology Conference*, Salt Lake City, UT, May 2001, http://www.stc-online.org/.

11. R. Radice, "One on One," *High Quality Low Cost Software Inspections*, pp. 14-416–14-419.

12. R.T. McCann, "The Efficiency of Using Process Control Charts to Drive the Defect Prevention Process," *Software Productivity Consortium's Annual Member Forum*, Oct. 1999.

13. F. Shull et al., "Lab Package for the Empirical Investigation of Perspective-Based Reading," http://www.cs.umd.edu/projects/SoftEng/ESEG/manual/pbr_package/manual.html.

Chapter 5:
Residual Defect Estimation

One of the long-standing issues with any quality system is in estimating residual defects. How do we know whether or not we have more defects to find? As it happens, this question is very similar to the problem faced by the National Parks Service in estimating the numbers of various animals in Yellowstone National Park before and after the reintroduction of the Gray Wolf. One cannot count all deer or rabbits in the entire park at a single point in time. One must infer the total populations by sampling, tagging, and re-sampling, followed by the creative use of statistics.

When the capture-recapture model is applied to inspections, it is possible directly to derive an estimate of escaped defects. Let f_k be the number of defects found by exactly "k" inspectors acting independently. Then the number of escaped defects is best estimated as follows (see Figure 5-1):

$$E_{C-R} = M - U(m_j) = f_1 * [\sum (f_k)] / [\sum (k*f_k)]$$

$$\text{All } j \quad k \geq 1 \quad k > 1$$

Equation 27

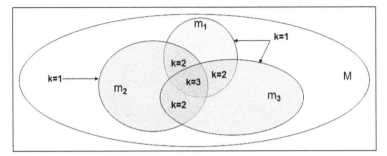

Figure 5-1. Venn diagram for the Capture-Recapture Model

This is not the only estimator available. If the results of the inspection team as a whole are tracked over time, an average performance emerges. That can then be used independently to estimate escaped defects:

$$E_A = [\underline{S} \cdot (-\underline{m})] * I * R$$

Equation 28

where

I = historical defect density (test + inspection)
$\underline{S}$ = size of inspected work (vector model)
$\underline{m}$ = slope of regression surface
R = inspection preparation rate

It is also possible to derive multiple estimates with existing parametric models such as QUALCOMO[1] or the Rayleigh estimation in SWEEP.[2]

If there are multiple estimates of the effectiveness of a quality practice available, they can be compared via standard hypothesis testing—for instance, by comparing the average performance of a whole inspection team to the average performance of an individual inspector. Another pair-wise comparison would be to compare the results and average performance of two or more independent defect capture methods, e.g., inspection vs. testing.

1   QUALCOMO is a variant of COCOMO II that models defect density. See B. Boehm et al., *Software Cost Estimation with COCOMO II*, Prentice-Hall, 2009.

2   SWEEP stands for SoftWare Error Estimation Program. See J. Gaffney, *The Software Measurement Guidebook*, Thomson Computer Press, 1995.

If statistically significant differences are found, then appropriate reme-dial actions can be taken, e.g., further inspection or testing. If a pattern of significant differences emerges from the analysis, then investigation of root causes and application of preventive actions may be appropriate.

It is also possible and often desirable to combine multiple estimates in the standard way to produce an improved estimate. In that case, simply use estimated standard deviation to compute the weighted average:

$$E = (E_{C-R} / S_{C-R} + E_A/S_A + \dots) / (1/S_{C-R} + 1/S_A + \dots)$$

It is clearly technically straightforward to estimate the residual error load after each quality practice and, indeed, just prior to system delivery. Organi-zationally it may be a different story altogether.

Friendly Caveat: Serious Management Support Required

a. Identifying and validating causes of variation is best done in the pres-ence of institutionalized CMMI Maturity Level 4 behavior (M&A CL 4, OPP, QPM)

b. Optimizing a causal model is best done in the presence of institution-alized CMMI Maturity Level 5 behavior (M&A CL 5, CAR, OID)

The key enabler is the willingness and ability to measure across organiza-tional and financial boundaries.[3]

Setting Expectations

As with any proposal to change human behavior, it is necessary to consid-er the natural human resistance to change. Chapter 6 of Machiavelli's *The Prince* contains an observation that still applies 500 years later. It is truly a timeless statement of the human condition:

> There is nothing more difficult to plan, more doubtful of
> success, nor more dangerous to manage than the creation of a
> new system. For the initiator has the enmity of all who would
> profit by the preservation of the old institutions and merely
> lukewarm defenders in those who would gain by the new ones.

---

3   See B. Boehm et al., *Software Cost Estimation with COCOMO II*, Prentice-Hall, 2009.

The hesitation of the latter arises in part…from the general skepticism of mankind, which does not really believe in an innovation until experience proves its value.
—Niccolo Machiavelli, 1513, in *The Prince*, Chapter 6

As an example, consider "Cost Plus" acquisition contracting (http://en.wikipedia.org/wiki/Cost-plus_pricing). With respect to the concepts in this monograph, the first question to ask is "who pays for rework"? In the Cost Plus strategy the customer pays for all developmental costs and provides an incentive for "good performance." If rework is categorized as a developmental cost, the customer pays for rework. If, in addition, the contractual incentives are primarily a combination of schedule and cost performance, then there is a clear disincentive to contain rework costs. Indeed, under these conditions, poor quality will look suspiciously like future sales to a business executive, and there will be little reason to support high-quality developmental practices that take advantage of the model developed in this work. The natural consequence of not containing rework at every step of the development will be to drive unpredicted variance into both cost and schedule due to increased rework—likely both late and over-budget per the generic prediction of this model.

In the Cost Plus arena, creation of suitable incentives that minimize total cost of ownership while minimizing cost and schedule variance and minimizing rework is a bit like attempting to carry a large bowl of Jell-O (http://brands.kraftfoods.com/jello) across a crowded dance floor – without the bowl. To achieve goals of this kind using this model, first eliminate rework by making cost and schedule accurately and precisely predictable, then manage the remaining causes of cost and schedule variance using a combination of analysis of variance together with root cause analysis and continuous process improvement.

Friendly advice:

Before attempting this kind of business transformation, first make sure you can answer the following questions from executives:

- "You mean to tell me you want me to spend profit dollars to cut revenue?"[4]

---

4   W. Humphrey, "Why Can't We Manage Large Projects," *CrossTalk*, July 2010, p. 11, http://www.crosstalkonline.org/storage/issue-archives/2010/201007/201007-Humphrey.pdf (as of 10/10/2011).

(N.B.: The definition of revenue may differ between the program and executive levels in an organization, so the calculation of return on investment will differ as well. Legal and contractual constraints will also differ across various sectors of the economy. All of these factors must be understood and factored into the calculations.)

- "If we perform this kind of measurement and analysis of business performance, per the US Truth in Negotiations Act[5] we will have to disclose it to the Government on all relevant US Federal contract proposals. Given the Darleen Druyen case[6] and the reality of corporate espionage,[7] it is reasonable to expect that our competitors will end up with the information. The only way to be certain our competitors don't get the information is to not collect it in the first place. Why would I want to collect and analyze such information?" [Answer: The competitive loss of not doing it compared to a competitor who does results in lost market share, as was experienced by the US Consumer Electronics and Automotive industries from the 1970s through the end of the century—but who has 30-year plans these days, or even 10-year plans?]

5   *US Truth in Negotiations Act*, 10 USC § 2306a, 41 USC § 254b, http://financial-dictionary.thefreedictionary.com/Truth+in+Negotiations+Act (as of 5/11/2011).

6   "Articles about Darleen A. Druyun," *New York Times*, http://topics.nytimes.com/topics/reference/timestopics/people/d/darleen_a_druyun/index.html, and "Darleen Druyun," *Wikipedia*, http://en.wikipedia.org/wiki/Darleen_Druyun (both as of 5/10/2011).

7   "A couple of old, but interesting articles regarding how Boeing was caught in acts of corporate espionage against their rival, Lockheed Martin, and more," blog, 18 Oct. 2008, http://whistleblowersupporter.typepad.com/my_weblog/2008/10/a-couple-of-old-but-interesting-articles-regarding-how-boeing-was-caught-in-acts-of-corporate-espionage-against-their-riva.html, and L. Wayne, "Chief Executive At Boeing Quits Under Criticism," New York Times, 2 Dec. 2003, http://www.nytimes.com/2003/12/02/business/02BOEI.html?pagewanted=all (as of 5/11/2011).

Making effective use of this model requires real commitment and invest-ment in culture change. These, while competitively necessary, are often hard to come by, but once accomplished, this model creates a barrier to competition because its use directly supports continuous process improvement that, once begun, is hard for competitors to match and overtake.

Culture change has always been a difficult endeavor, see the Machia-velli quote above. There have been many good books written on how to accomplish this. The following is a short list of very good ones:

Frederick Winslow Taylor, *Principles of Scientific Management*
Kim Caputo, *CMM Implementation Guide*
Michael Hammer and James Conway, *Reengineering the Corporation*
Alexandra Shackleton et al., *Shackleton's Way*
Gary P. Ferraro, *Cultural Dimensions in International Business*
Miyamoto Mushashi, *The Book of Five Rings*
Sun Tzu, *The Art of War*, trans. Samuel B. Griffith and B. H. Liddell Hart.

At the highest level of abstraction, there are a few basic steps that are necessary:

- Identify a sponsor among executive management (preferably the Presi-dent or CEO or other C-officer)
- Identify a champion—the operational manager who will oversee the de-sign and operation of the change design and implementation teams—the person who is responsible for getting it done
- Identify goals that directly support the strategic plan
- Create a clear transition plan with clear tracking milestones and sup-porting metrics that demonstrate added value
- Socialize the intent of the change and grow buy-in among the employees
- Destabilize the existing culture
- Motivate and reward desirable change
- Stabilize the intended culture
- Celebrate progress

Related articles published

1. "How Much Code Inspection Is Enough?" *CrossTalk*, July 2001, http://www.crosstalkonline.org/storage/issue-archives/2001/200107/200107-McCann.pdf.
2. "When Is It Cost Effective to Use Formal Software Inspections?" *CrossTalk*, Mar. 2004, http://www.crosstalkonline.org/storage/issue-archives/2004/200403/200403-McCann.pdf.
3. "The Relative Cost of Interchanging, Adding, or Dropping Quality Practices," *CrossTalk*, June 2007, http://www.crosstalkonline.org/storage/issue-archives/2007/200706/200706-McCann.pdf.

References

1. A. Chao, S.M. Lee, and S.L. Jeng, "Estimating Population Size for Capture-Recapture Data When Capture Probabilities Vary by Time and Individual Animal," *Biometrics*, vol. 48, no. 1, Mar. 1992, pp. 201–216.
2. M.G. Fagan, "Design and Code Inspections to Reduce Errors in Program Development," *IBM Systems Journal*, vol. 15, no. 3, 1976.
3. M.G. Fagan, "Advances in Software Inspections," *IEEE Transactions on Software Engineering*, vol. SE-12, no. 7, July 1986.
4. "COQUALMO," June 2009, http://csse.usc.edu/csse/research/COQUALMO/.
5. J. Gaffney on the Software Error Estimation Program (SWEEP), discussed in C. Smith and C. Uber, "Experience Report on Early Software Reliability Prediction and Estimation," *10th International Symposium on Software Reliability Engineering (ISSRE)*, IEEE Computer Society, 1999, p. 282, http://www.computer.org/portal/web/csdl/doi/10.1109/ISSRE.1999.809333.
6. G. Roedler, R. Valerdi, J. Fortune, J. Gaffney, and D.J. Reifer, "Harmonizing Software and Systems Engineering Cost Estimation" *23rd International Forum on COCOMO(TM) and System/Software Cost Modeling and ICM Workshop 3*, 27 Oct. 2008, http://sunset.usc.edu/csse/event/2008/cocomoicm08/pages/program.html; http://sunset.usc.edu/csse/event/2008/cocomoicm08/presentationByDay/Mon_Oct27/10_Harmonizing%20SE%20&%20SW%20Estimation%20-%20For%20COCOMO%20Forum%20-%20GJR.ppt.

www.ingramcontent.com/pod-product-compliance
Lightning Source LLC
Chambersburg PA
CBHW060458060326
40689CB00020B/4573